Dare to Dream Again!

What if your dreams are waiting on you?
All that's left for you is to take the first step.

CHARLES MAXELL, JR.

Published by
Charles Maxell, Jr. Consulting Group LLC
Smyrna, Georgia
Printed in the United States of America
First edition
For information, permissions, or bulk purchases, contact:
Charles Maxell, Jr. Consulting Group LLC
Audio Book ISBN: 979-8-9938936-3-1
Ebook ISBN: 979-8-9938936-2-4
Paperback ISBN: 979-8-9938936-4-8
Hardback ISBN: 979-8-9938936-0-0

Table of Contents

Praise for
Dare to Dream Again!

"Pastor Charles Maxell gives an insightful critique and profound theological thought on classic biblical text, while offering practical directives on faith and confidence in transitional times.

This book is riveted with colorful illustrations and cultural interpretations that shape how we see the world around us, more importantly, how we can apply faith and hope that sustains through changing times. While providing solid exegetical perspectives of scripture, this book also enhances the lens for which we understand and interpret the inconveniences of life, while also providing serious directives for transformation in the Kingdom of God.

This book will enhance your vision, leadership, passion, coping skills, and life survival techniques. This is a flawless work, and a must read!"

Bishop Sir Walter Mack
Union Baptist Church
Winston-Salem, NC

"Pastor Charles Maxell writes from a well of experience as a dreamer. However, Maxell's admonition to dream again is also rooted in the truth of Biblical witness. In "Dare to Dream Again!" readers will know that dreaming is not a fanatical wish but is an innate drive that connects God's purpose with God's destiny. Maxell's passionate and practical motivation will birth believers who take the risk to dream again."

Tyshawn Gardner, PhD
Associate Professor of Preaching
Holder of the David E. Garland Endowed Chair in Preaching
Baylor University, George w. Truett Theological Seminary

""Dare to Dream Again!" perfectly blends practical steps with Biblical truth in a way that feels approachable and encouraging. Charles' voice is relatable and familiar. His words read like one sermon you know immediately is for you, supportive and direct but never preachy. I closed the book reminded of my dreams and ready to do something about them. It's an inspiring and practical guide for anyone ready to move forward with faith and confidence."

Elaine Armstrong
VP, Marketing
Goodwill of North Georgia

"Charles Maxell, Jr. has written more than a book, he's issued a raw, transparent, and actionable call to every soul stuck in the in-between. "Dare to Dream Again!" challenges you to want more, do more, and become more, starting not someday, but right now. It reminds us that Haran is not our home, and the dream isn't dead, it's just waiting on our yes. This book shakes the dust-off dormant visions and dares you to believe that your next chapter can be bolder, braver, and more purposeful than anything behind you. If you've ever felt stuck, settled, or silenced, this is your wake-up call and your breakthrough blueprint."

Chris Cooper
Executive Peak Performance & Business Results Coach, Speaker, Trainer and 2xs #1 Best Selling Author

"Charles Maxell, Jr.'s "Dare to Dream Again!" is a powerful and timely reflection on embracing uncertainty, setting bold visions, and leading with courage. This book is a timely resource for anyone seeking to inspire change, whether in business or life. I have known Charles for years and heard him deliver the original sermons that inspired this book. His advice to "go even when you don't have all the answers" sustains me as I lead our mission-driven company through growing pains and a rapidly changing environment. I deeply respect Charles' authentic reflections and the proven results he's achieved as a spiritual and corporate leader. "Dare to Dream Again!" is for anyone ready to trust in a greater future."

Robert James, II
CEO, Carver Financial Corporation
Immediate Past Chairman, National Bankers Association

"Dare to Dream Again!" isn't really a choice. There isn't an "or" at the end of the change. Instead, it's a dare you must take to discover the truth of realizing the potential God has placed in your life. This written conversation with Rev. Charles A. Maxell, Jr. reminds us to listen to the call of our hearts and spirits, and to abandon the siren song of comfort that often traps us between where we are and where we are "purpose-made" to be. Maxell leaves you laughing (with a few "no, he didn't say that" moments) and inspired to face forward and take the next steps toward your own dream. My first thought when I finished was, "I can't wait to pass this one to someone I love."

Sara Prince
Senior Partner, McKinsey

"Dare to Dream Again!" is more than a book, it's a spiritual awakening. Through Scripture, storytelling, and soul-stirring insight, Charles Maxell, Jr. helps you believe that your greatest days are not behind you, but ahead of you. This book offers a powerful reminder that God's promises are still alive, and so are our dreams."

Pastor Tony Lee
Senior Pastor
Community of Hope AME Church
Washington, D.C.

DEDICATED

To my parents, **Rev. Bernese Shaw** *and* **Rev. Dr. Charles A. Maxell, Sr.**

Thank you for introducing me to the resurrection power of Jesus Christ, for the gift of imagination and for the examples of resiliency and grit that have taught me that my dreams are always possible.

6 Direct your children onto the right path, and when they are older, they will not leave it.¹

FOREWORD

God has visions for our lives that are greater than visions we may have for ourselves, or others may have for us. One of the disconcerting aspects of God's vision is that they are sometimes disconcerting and unsettling compared to perceptions we may have had for ourselves, our careers, and the institutions and cultures we have seen as our primary life work. Reverend Charles Maxell, Jr. is a primary example and embodiment of the of the unsettling nature of God's visions and plans for our lives.

Reverend Maxell epitomized the reality of success as a senior executive and trusted advisor to Fortune 500 companies. A number of his colleagues and persons he superintended would be content to do what he did and become who and what he became in their own business careers.

However, despite his track-record, knowledge and contacts in the business insurance industry, he felt a restlessness, a fire he could not quench, and the visionary stirrings of God for the ordained ministry of word and sacrament beyond the noble function of either a pulpit associate or a traditional institutional pastor. Reverend Maxell and his wife Jennifer Elaine, his partner in ministry, felt moved by the Holy Spirit to organize a congregation of believers with an emphasis on de-churched persons or individuals who were victims of church hurt.

The truth that many believers wrestle with, though we rarely name it aloud, is that some churches, tragically, can be places of harm. Instead of lifting people up, they break them down. Where there should be clarity, confusion reigns. Where there should be healing, wounds linger. Churches meant to minister, nurture, and empower sometimes distort their purpose, leaving members exploited, lied to, and misused. It is one of the most painful realities a person of faith can face, even more wounding than betrayal by family or friends.

As David lamented, *"It is not enemies who taunt me. I could bear that...But it is you, my equal, my companion, my familiar friend, with whom I kept pleasant company we walked in the house of God with the throng."*[2] Such wounds run deep. Some, hurt beyond measure, leave the church and never return. Others stay sometimes out of loyalty, family bonds, or a sense of obligation, but their hearts grow bitter, joyless, and distant. Still others remain present yet uninvolved, keeping their gifts and passions hidden, wary of being vulnerable again.

These responses: bitterness, withdrawal, self-protection are not signs of spiritual weakness, but reminders of real pain inflicted by trusted companions in sacred space. Yet even as we recognize these patterns, we must also remember you can love the Lord, remain in the church, and still carry the marks of church hurt.

This book arrives at a moment when many, perhaps you as well, are carrying invisible burdens, nursing spiritual wounds, or standing at the threshold of surrendering hope. Charles and Jennifer Elaine, his partner in life and ministry, have devoted their work to inviting back those who have been driven away or diminished by broken systems, offering space for restoration and a path toward rediscovering faith and purpose.

In the pages that follow, you will not merely find yourself recounting the hurts or flaws within the church, you will be invited into a larger narrative, one in which every loss and wound can serve as the soil for new beginnings. "Dare to Dream Again" is more than a call to action. It's a roadmap for transformation. This book will show you, through the lens of Biblical stories and lived testimony, how God specializes in rewriting our endings into beginnings and our pain into purpose.

But most of all, you will come to see, as Reverend Maxell has, that your story is unfinished. There are new dreams waiting to be birthed from the ashes of old disappointments. Each chapter offers not only honest acknowledgement of brokenness but, even more, practical guidance, prayerful encouragement, and spiritual tools to move from wounds to wholeness and resignation to vibrant hope.

No matter if someone is a victim of career abuse, family abuse, relationship or friendship abuse, we are grateful for Reverend Maxell's declaration to "Dare to Dream Again!" Not only does Reverend Maxell encourage us to "Dare to Dream Again" he also equips us with the steps and counsel for transforming our past hurts with present healing, our past brokenness with present breakthroughs, our past pain with present perseverance, and our past rejections with present redemption and resurrections. Thank you, Reverend Maxell, for encouraging, equipping and empowering us to "Dare to Dream Again," no matter who we are, how old we are, or what our history has been ---whether sorrowful or splendiferous.

Reader, let this be your invitation, not only to remember the dreams you once cherished, but to expect that God is already preparing something even greater. Transformation and hope are not theoretical, but real and available, as you take each step in faith. The same God who called Reverend Maxell beyond comfort and convention calls you, even now, to imagine, to believe, and to trust that your greatest days of purpose may yet be before you.

Thank you, Reverend Maxell for reminding us that even if we are in our eighties like Moses, with an active murder warrant over our heads, we can "Dare to Dream Again," and become God's liberator for an oppressed people who have been in slavery for over 400 years. Thank you, Reverend Maxell for reminding us that when, like the prophet Elijah, we are fearful, depressed and lonely, we can "Dare to Dream Again," and continue to pursue God's vision for our lives with resources we were not aware we had. Thank you, Reverend Maxell for reminding us that even when, like Ruth, we are reeling and rocking with bereavement, sorrow and an uncertain future, we can "Dare to Dream Again," and discover that our latter days will be greater than our former days.

Thank you, Reverend Maxell for reminding us that even when, like Mary Magdelene, we are dismissed because of our painful, emotional history and stress, we can "Dare to Dream Again," and become a close follower and major influence in the life and ministry of none other than the Lord Jesus Christ. Thank you, Reverend Maxell, for reminding us that, like Saul of Tarsus, we can "Dare to Dream Again," and become a new creation like the Apostle Paul, a leading church founder and author of Scripture. Thank you, Reverend Maxell for reminding us, that when we follow the Lord Jesus Christ, we can "Dare to Dream Again," and his words can become our testimony and our legacy, "Very truly, I tell you, the one who believes in me will also do the works that I do and, in fact, will do greater works than these, because I am going to the Father."[3]

My prayer is that as you read this book, you will sense a gentle nudge, a signpost, reminding you that healing, renewal, and unimaginable transformation are closer than you think.

Thank you, Reverend Charles Alexander Maxell, Jr., for "Daring to Dream Again," because your example, your ministry, your witness, and your life embody the hope and the help, the vision and the victory, and the dreams and the destiny promised to us in the Scriptures: *"See what love the Father has given us, that we should be called children of God, and that is what we are. The reason the world does not know us is that it did not know him. Beloved, we are God's children now; what we will be, has not yet been revealed. What we do know is this: when he is revealed, we will be like him, for we will see him as he is."*[4]

William D. Watley, Ph.D.
Fall, 2025

Introduction
Is it possible to dream again?

Remember when you were a child? Remember when the world was a blank sheet of paper, a bare canvas, and your dreams were as endless as the stars in the sky? Maybe you wanted to be an astronaut, a professional athlete, a supreme court judge, a movie actor, an inventor or the President of the United States. Back then, nothing seemed impossible. You built castles out of cardboard, sailed pirate ships in your backyard, took the game winning shot to win an NBA championship on the old rusty basketball goal with no net, and believed that tomorrow could bring endless possibilities. But then, life happened.

Disappointments crept in like shadows at dusk. Responsibilities piled up. Maybe you lost someone you loved, or a door you desperately wanted to open, slammed shut in your face. Somewhere along the way, you stopped dreaming. And the world, once so full of color and contrast, faded to gray. You settled for what was safe, what was expected, and what was "good enough."

The reason I know about this condition is because the shadows in my own life have crept in. Life responsibilities have piled up. I have lost someone I loved and I have had a few doors shut in my face. As I write these words, I am standing at my own crossroads.

For the first time in three decades, I found myself without a job. My carefully crafted plans, scattered like leaves in a Fall wind. I've watched others walk this road, but I never thought it would be me. My life was supposed to follow a script, steady progress and predictable success. But the last few years have been anything but predictable success. Some dreams withered. Some hopes slipped through my fingers. And some visions I once held with such clarity are now blurry outlines in the distance.

Don't get me wrong, I have known success. I've been married longer than my parents. My amazing wife has blessed me with three wonderful, bright and talented children. I've worked at major corporations and have traveled the world, closing deals and conducting business at the highest level. I've built a church from scratch. I sit on boards and am considered a civic and community leader. And like some of you, I survived September 11, 2001, and a global pandemic. In so many ways, I'm rich, blessed and highly favored. But if I'm honest with myself, it's not the kind of success I once dreamed of. I saw myself as a CEO, or a major pastor of a big-time church, or an influential voice on the national and the world stage.

Maybe my dreams were too lofty. Maybe they were unrealistic. In any case, there are moments I feel like Abram's father, Terah, in Genesis 11:31: *Terah took his son Abram, his grandson Lot son of Haran, and his daughter-in-law Sarai, the wife of his son Abram, and together they set out from Ur of the Chaldeans to go to Canaan. But when they came to Haran, they settled there."5*

I know my feelings of unactualized goals are more in my head than reality. And I know there are hundreds, maybe thousands of people, who would love my life and my success. Yet for me, there were moments in my life that I felt like I was in Haran --- somewhere between where I started and where I hoped to be. **That's what Haran is. It's the theoretical, yet real, halfway point in our lives. The place where dreams go to sleep and struggle to wake up.**

The Bible says that Abram's family set out for the land of promise, but for some reason, they stopped short. They settled. And that one decision changed everything. The journey paused. The promise delayed. Haran became more than a place. Haran became a mindset, a holding pattern, a place of comfort but also a place of compromise.

I know what it's like to settle in Haran. I know what it's like to wake up each morning with a dull ache of unfulfillment. I know what it's like to scroll through social media and feel a pang of envy instead of joy at the success of others. I know what it's like to mourn for a life I wanted to live but never fully achieved. My Haran was a place where I convinced myself that "good enough" was all I could expect. A place where fear and doubt whispered that my dreams were too big, too late, too much. There are so many things I still want to do, can do, and should do. But something is holding me back. "Why," I ask myself, "am I still in Haran?"

Yet, after one restless night, I looked in the mirror and said, "Enough." Enough of settling. Enough of making excuses. Enough of feeling sorry for myself. If I wanted a different life, then I had to create a different life. And in that moment, like Abram, I heard God's call, and I decided to answer. Even though I have no idea where this new path will take me, I believe it's going to take me somewhere beyond settling. Somewhere closer to the promise. Somewhere I can dare to dream again.

Even writing this book has been a journey. Fourteen years ago, Genesis 11:31 caught my attention and stirred a series of thoughts deep within me. I scribbled ideas in journals, jotted notes on napkins, and dreamed of writing a book. But I never thought I had something to say that was worth reading. So, I let that dream sit on a shelf, gathering dust until now. I still have doubts. And maybe what you are to read will seem elementary to you. Yet, today, I am finally putting pen to paper, not because I have all the answers, but because I am daring to believe that my story, and yours, still matters.

This book is for anyone who finds themselves in the in-between: longing for hope, searching for purpose, wanting to do more, be more impactful, aching to rediscover the courage to dream again. Along the way, we will explore:

- **Second Chances and New Beginnings:** Life is too precious to settle. And if you don't give up, life offers fresh starts, second chances and new beginnings, even after deep disappointments.

- **Faith over Fear:** Faith is not the absence of fear. Faith is choosing to trust God's vision, even when the road is hard to see and the way ahead is hidden by fog.

- **Resiliency and Grit**: One of the great lessons of life is learning that dreams are often realized on the other side of through.

- **Personal and Spiritual Growth**: Embracing the transformation that comes with pursuing your God given dreams.

- **Purpose Beyond Self:** Discovering that your dreams are meant not just for you, but to bless others and make a difference in the world.

- **Practical Steps:** No matter where you start, gaining tools, hearing stories and receiving encouragement to take actionable steps toward your dreams.

Using the call of Abram as our canvas, and drawing from my own journey, as well as the real-life stories of others who have dared to trust God, this book explores how living by faith transforms empty spaces into places of hope, opens doors to new horizons, and empowers you to claim the future that God has prepared for you. Even when you cannot see it.

These pages are alive with sermons I have preached and lessons I have learned in this journey called life. Lessons I learned with sometimes trembling hands and sometimes with tear-stained notes. So, don't be surprised if you hear a "here is your shout!" or "y'all ain't talking back to me" folded in the recipe of this work. Every chapter is crafted to evoke an emotion, ignite your hope, call you to action and propel you forward.

If you have ever felt stuck in Haran, or wondered if it's too late to dream again, this is your invitation to leave the halfway point behind. It's not too late. Come on. Let's dare to dream again!

CHAPTER 1
What Got You Here Won't Get You There

Genesis 11:27-32[6]
Descendants of Terah

27 Now these are the descendants of Terah. Terah was the father of Abram, Nahor, and Haran, and Haran was the father of Lot. 28 Haran died before his father Terah in the land of his birth, in Ur of the Chaldeans. 29 Abram and Nahor took wives; the name of Abram's wife was Sarai, and the name of Nahor's wife was Milcah. She was the daughter of Haran the father of Milcah and Iscah. 30 Now Sarai was barren; she had no child.

31 Terah took his son Abram and his grandson Lot son of Haran and his daughter-in-law Sarai, his son Abram's wife, and they went out together from Ur of the Chaldeans to go into the land of Canaan, but when they came to Haran, they settled there. 32 The days of Terah were two hundred five years, and Terah died in Haran.

In this thing called life, you will always be in transit from "HERE" to "THERE." HERE can be a great place, a fruitful place. HERE is a place where you can be CEO of a thriving company. HERE is the place where you are working and discovering the potential that is growing inside of you. HERE is the place where you are looking good and feeling fine and where everything you touch turns to gold. HERE is the place where dreams are born, and partnerships are formed. HERE is a comfortable place, a convenient place, and a familiar place on the road to THERE.

THERE is where you want to go. THERE is the place you want to be. THERE is the place where you can be a CEO who is viewed as a great leader because you have a vested interest in everyone's success and treat everyone with respect. THERE is the place where the labor and the sacrifice may be hard, but you know that you have something inside of you worth pushing for, worth fighting for, worth sacrificing for, worth delivering.

THERE is the place where your life is not measured by what you have. THERE is the place where your life is valued by what you give. THERE is not a place of New Year's Resolutions. THERE is a place of transformative and life changing events that make you a better person, a better wife, a better husband, a better mother, a better father and a better friend.

Trace your own personal map. You are HERE. You're talented. You're smart. You're young. You're full of potential and energy and hope and ambition.

You are HERE. You're experienced. You're tested. You've been there. You've done that. But you still want to get to THERE...to the Promised Land...to the vision that God has for your life. But hear me when I say this: what got you HERE won't get you THERE.

Your good looks got you HERE. But it's going to take more than a cute butt and a smile to get you THERE. Your pedigree got you HERE. But it's going to take more than a name and a phone call to get you THERE. Your fasting may help you lose a few pounds on the scale. But continual patterns of healthy eating and rest and exercise are needed to get you a healthier and stronger you. You are HERE. You want to get THERE. But what got you here, won't get you THERE.

That's the lesson that we learn from Terah. The bible says: *27 Now these are the descendants of Terah. Terah was the father of Abram, Nahor, and Haran, and Haran was the father of Lot...31 Terah took his son Abram and his grandson Lot son of Haran and his daughter-in-law Sarai, his son Abram's wife, and they went out together from Ur of the Chaldeans to go into the land of Canaan, but when they came to Haran,* **they settled there.**7

Have you ever wondered why people with so much potential, and energy and talent and hope and ambition often settle for less than

what God wanted for their lives? Why do people on the precipice of something big abort their visions too soon? Why, I wondered, with all the family support and provisions and vision of where he wanted to do, did Terah settle in Haran before reaching his final destination? I believe there are many reasons why, but I submit to you three.

I confess that one of the biggest challenges of pastoring is dealing with what people hold on to. They have one bad memory, and all churches are the same. They have one bad experience and all pastors are crooks. They fall out with one person and all the church folks are suspicious. But I came to tell someone that you will never get something new, while holding on to something old.

You will never get a fresh anointing, holding on to old anger. You will never get a new breakthrough, holding on to yesterday's bitterness. You will never get a new beginning, holding onto old burdens. Some things you must let go.

Maybe for Terah, Haran reminded him of his son that shared the same name. Maybe that's why Terah settled in Haran. He couldn't let go. Maybe he couldn't stop remembering what he left. Maybe he couldn't stop remembering what he lost.

Verse 28 says that "Haran died before his father Terah in the land of his birth..." Maybe the pain of losing his son became too much for Terah to handle. Maybe the constant reminder of his name was comforting and somewhat consoling. **But the tragedy of clinging to things that are gone is that you will never discover the new things that God is bringing your way.** The prophet Isaiah recorded God's words this way: *"Do not remember the former things or consider the things of old. I am about to do a new thing..."*[8]

The bible doesn't implicitly say it, but Terah wasn't an ordinary Joe. While he faced tragedy in his life, the loss of his son and the barrenness of his daughter-in-law Sarai, he could trace his lineage back to Adam and Eve. Maybe that's why Terah settled in Haran. He suffered from the issue that a lot of overachievers suffer from. He suffered from: winning too much and sometimes winning too soon.

Now before you dismiss my claim as cliché, consider this. This is where a lot of us are. We achieved success early in life. We went to college. We got a job. We started a family and began to ascend the economic and social ladder. We achieved all the trappings of success.

We have the house. We have the car. We have the title. We have achieved things, and we have done much. But we quickly discover that what got us here won't get us there. Talent is good, but talent alone is not enough to compete in this new economy. Ambition is good, but ambition without favor won't get you the next promotion. Potential and hope are good, but the phone company and the bank don't accept them as currency to pay your bills. "Why not?" We ask. It worked before. You won before. You thrived before. Winning was easy back in the day. Talent was all you needed. Luck was all you needed. Ambition was all you needed. But that was then, and this is now. Now instead of accumulating wins on our score column, some of our box scores record more losses and setbacks than victories and successes. Is this your story?

For Terah, this message is too little, too late. Because the bible says in verse 32: *"The days of Terah were two hundred five years; and Terah died in Haran."* And when Terah died, all his dreams and hopes died too.

Yet, I believe Terah's fate doesn't have to be your story. In fact, I have three strategies to help you get from "HERE" to "THERE."

Strategy 1: You will never reach your destiny, walking in someone else's vision.

We read of Terah and his family leaving Ur at the end of Genesis 11. Then in the next chapter, we read of God's great promise to Terah's son, Abram. In many English translations it looks as if the promise was made after they had left Ur. Yet Stephen's speech to the Sanhedrin, as found in Acts 7:2-4, gives us a different timeline. In the text, you will find these words:

²And Stephen replied: "Brothers[ω] and fathers, listen to me. The God of glory appeared to our ancestor Abraham when he was in Mesopotamia, before he lived in Haran, ³ and said to him, 'Leave your country and your relatives and go to the land that I will show you.' ⁴ Then he left the country of the Chaldeans and settled in Haran. After his father died, God had him move from there to this country in which you are now living.⁹

When you study the text closely, you will discover that the tense of the verb in some of the more literal translations suggests that the promise was made while they were still in Ur. In fact, God came to Abram while they were in Ur, telling him to leave Ur, and to move to Canaan, a land that he would give to him and his descendants. The one true God promised Abram that he would be his, that he would use him to bless the whole world, and that his home would be in Canaan.

As was the custom in the culture, Abram would have told his father. And Terah, in obedience to the call, the command, the promise of God, would have left Ur and set off for Canaan.

In some respects, Terah showed remarkable faith. Without warning and without Google maps, Terah was willing to leave everything he knew based upon a promise. A promise from a God he didn't know and a promise from God he didn't worship. A promise made to his son, and not to him.

The bible says Terah's journey of obedience started so well. He set out for Canaan, full of obedience and hope and faith and expectation. But the bible says he settled in Haran, never reaching his final destination.

Let this be a cautionary tale to someone. **You can never reach your destiny, walking in someone else's vision.** Don't get me wrong. I'm not saying that you can't believe in a cause you didn't originate or find your life's calling in the vision that someone else has presented. But in the midst of doing so, the vision must become yours.

Maybe that's why Terah settled in Haran. The vision to go to Canaan wasn't his. It was Abram's. He tried. He wanted to support his son. He wanted to be a good father. He wanted to believe in God's promises and God's provision. But Haran was a familiar place.

Haran was smaller but similar to Ur. It had similar customs, similar culture and worshipped similar gods. Maybe Terah said to himself, "God's promise sounds good, but this is what I know. This is how I see my life."

When I was a little boy, my father didn't have visions of me becoming a pastor. He desperately wanted me to become a doctor. In his mind, that was a career that guaranteed success and fame and a potential for generational wealth. And for a while, I tried my best to live up to that dream. I read books on medicine. I studied chemistry, biology, and math in high school and college. My senior project for high school was on the effects of stress on the heart in athletes versus nonathletes. I told myself and I told others that I wanted to be a doctor.

While I found medicine interesting, I hated chemistry. I hated biology. I made mediocre grades at best and eventually discovered that economic theory and finance and Greek mythology were my true loves. And here is the funny thing, the site of needles makes me anxious and queasy. Not the characteristics that you want from your doctor.

I had the desire. I had the will. I even had the motivation to make my father proud. But all that wasn't going to get me through medical school or make me a good doctor.

I don't know who this word is for, but I speak from experience, you will never reach your destiny walking in someone else's vision. God has a unique and specific vision just for your life. If you haven't heard it, wait on it. If you don't know when you hear it, pray that God will give you the ear to hear him clearly.

Strategy 2: When your comfort zone becomes uncomfortable, it's time to grow past it.

Let me give credit to my wife, Jennifer, for this point because when I heard her say it, my spirit got so excited I almost threw my shoe at her. If I had to define vision, **vision is a mental picture of what can be, fueled**

by a passion of what should be. In other words, you can't say you want to do the big things of God by doing the small things of the world.

Let me ask you a question. How much further along would you be if you stop wasting time on places that are too small for you? In my experience, tenacity is a virtue; but there are some things we need to let go. Complacency and mediocrity are often born out of the crucible of stubbornness.

The problem that a lot of us find ourselves in is that we have outgrown the box in which we have placed ourselves. We keep playing with folk who are not in our weight class. We keep dealing with folk who don't have the intellectual prowess that we have. We dummy ourselves down in order to fit in with folk who aren't talking about nothing. And as a result, this small mindedness has impacted our lives. We can't stretch our gifts. We can't exercise our abilities. We're confined to spaces and places that are below our station. And like Terah, we are slowly dying in a bed of mediocrity.

That's why, when the comfort zone becomes uncomfortable, it's time to grow past it. I know it's safe. I know it's familiar, but it doesn't fit anymore. It can't hold you. And it won't give you peace.

In this season of your life, God is getting ready to send you something bigger than you can hold. When you try to press it down it won't fit but overflows. God is getting ready to send you something beyond what you can manage. God is getting ready to pour into your life something that you don't have the experience to deal with.

I want to pause and say this to you: **something BIG is getting ready to happen for you.** How big, you ask? It's so BIG that eyes have not seen. Ears have not heard.[10] Do me a favor. Put the book down and lift up your hands. I want to say this over your life:

> *In the name of Jesus, I release over every lifted hand the anointing of Jabez. I prophesize that everything you've got is too small for you. God is getting ready to release something BIG in your life: a BIG door, a BIG opportunity, a BIG breakthrough. The Spirit is saying: "You have had enough small stuff. Something BIG is getting ready to happen for you."* AMEN!

And finally, Strategy #3: Don't expect others to take greater risks or make greater sacrifices than you.

Terah was the patriarch of the family. While the vision was given to Abram, he was the one who was the earthly protector, provider and sustainer of the family. The Bible says he took with him his family on a quest to fulfill the vision of reaching Canaan. But for some reason, Terah settled in Haran, never to reach his final destination. Why? We don't know.

Maybe for him, and maybe for you, the pain of sacrifice is greater than the pain of regret. But experience has taught me that there's something inauthentic about a man or a woman who casts a vision for which he or she is not willing to personally sacrifice to attain. I know what I just said sounds harsh but here's the reality: **real vision always demands real investment.** Did you hear what I just said? Real vision always demands real investment. Anybody can dream about what could be, but only the committed will sacrifice for what should be. That's why the call of God rarely comes with shortcuts. Instead, it comes with instructions like sacrifice and grit and resilience. So, before you shout about the next big thing, ask yourself: are you willing to walk through the valley as eagerly as you are willing to celebrate on the mountaintop? Because vision without sacrifice isn't faith, it's fantasy.

For some reason, known only to God, God has chosen to work through men and women who are willing to make sacrifices for the sake of the thing he has placed in their hearts to do. Search the scriptures. Search the pages of church history. You won't find an example of anyone that God used, in even a small way, who did not make some kind of sacrifice to pursue the vision.

I would be naïve to say that I understand completely why God operates this way. But one thing I do know. When a man or woman is willing to give up something valuable for a God-ordained vision, God looks upon it as worship. When we sacrifice to do the thing, God has put in our hearts to do, we are recognizing and responding to our greatness. We are in effect saying, "God, this vision is worth whatever sacrifice I need to make. And you are worthy of my allegiance."

That's how you get from here, to there. You stretch out on God.

That's just what Jesus did. After two and a half years of teaching and healing, Jesus found himself on the Mountain of Gethsemane. The Bible says Jesus prayed, *"Abba Father...with you all things are possible. Remove this bitter cup from me."*[11] Jesus wasn't afraid of the cross, for he knew what God's vision for his life was. The issue he had was that he knew bearing our sin would separate him from God. So, he cried out, *"Is there another way?"* But in his silence, God said *"In order for you to get from here to there, casting out demons is not going to do it. Healing the sick and the blind is not going to do it. Raising the dead is not going to do it. Walking on water is not going to do it. Performing miracles and preaching sermons is not going to do it. If you want to walk in the vision that I have for your life, you must bear the world's sin."* **That's what I love about Jesus. He would never settle for less than his best.** For the Bible says, wiping the tears from his face he cried out to God, *"...yet, not what I want, but what you want."*[12]

I don't know who this is for, but God has a vision for your life. But here's the challenge: to walk in God's vision for your life, you can't keep doing the same thing, the same way. Transformation doesn't happen by accident; it requires intentional change. Yet, if you dare to surrender to God's will, if you have the courage to obey God's word, and if you dare to trust God enough to do things differently, you will witness something amazing. The same God who spoke worlds into existence is able to do exceedingly, abundantly, more than you can ask or imagine. So, stand on His promises and declare with faith: there's nothing our God cannot do! No mountain He cannot move. No door He cannot open. Nothing is impossible, because there's nothing our God cannot do!

CHAPTER 2
Should I Stay, or Should I Go?

Genesis 11:31-12:2

31 Terah took his son Abram and his grandson Lot son of Haran and his daughter-in-law Sarai, his son Abram's wife, and they went out together from Ur of the Chaldeans to go into the land of Canaan, but when they came to Haran, they settled there. 32 The days of Terah were two hundred five years, and Terah died in Haran.

The Call of Abram

12 Now the Lord said to Abram, "Go from your country and your kindred and your father's house to the land that I will show you. 2 I will make of you a great nation, and I will bless you and make your name great, so that you will be a blessing.

Imagine standing at the precipice of a decision that will forever reshape the landscape of your life. The air is thick with anticipation, and the weight of uncertainty hangs heavy over your shoulders. This is where Abram stood, poised between the familiar comfort of Haran and the uncharted promise of Canaan, as God's call echoed through the silence: *"Leave your country, your people and your father's household and go to the land I will show you."*[13] In this moment, Abram is faced with a choice that would define his destiny: **"Should I stay, or should I go?[14]"**

I believe the question that resonated within him is one that still echoes through our own lives today. Should I stay, or should I go? **Should you stay** trapped in a 9-to-5 routine, yearning for a career that ignites your passions? Should you remain within the confines of familiarity or take bold steps towards your dreams, even if it means venturing into the unknown? Should you continue the well-trodden path of mediocrity, or seize those divine moments that beckon you towards greatness? Should you cling to the comfort of Haran, familiar, convenient, and safe, or boldly pursue the life that God has envisioned for you, even if it means letting go of the old and embracing the new? Should we continue to cling to the old and to the dead: old ways and dead relationships, or should we let them go to walk in the new visions that God has for our lives?

Abram's journey from Haran to Canaan is often lifted as a model of what it means to step out on God. The writer of **Hebrews 11:8-10** reminds us: *"[8] By faith, Abraham obeyed when he was called to set out for a place that he was to receive as an inheritance; and he set out, not knowing where he was going. [9] By* *faith he stayed for a time in the land that he had been promised, as in a foreign land, living in tents, as did Isaac and Jacob, who were heirs with him of the same promise. 10 For he looked forward to the city that has foundations, whose architect and builder is God."*

In the shadows of Abram's legendary journey to Canaan lies a lesser-known tale of his father, Terah. Genesis 11:31 reveals that Terah was the first to embark on this epic quest, taking his son Abram, grandson Lot, and daughter-in-law Sarai with him from Ur of the Chaldeans. Their destination was clear: the land of Canaan. Yet, fate had other plans. Upon reaching Haran, they settled, and Terah's dreams of Canaan were left unrealized. The final chapters of his life are summed up in a haunting phrase: *"he settles in Haran, and he died there."*[15]

I wonder how many of us can be honest and admit we are Terah? We started out well. We were enthusiastic. We were bold. We were risk takers. We were visionary. We were courageous. Then we came to Haran. Success came. Promotions came. Money came. Bills came. Mortgages and car notes came. The mundane and the routine came. Children came. Stress came. Responsibilities came. And like Terah, time goes by and we find ourselves stuck in the same place, doing the same thing, asking the same questions while the vision of Canaan fades into the distance and the memory of our purpose grows dim, lost in the haze of our daily lives.

The Bible says Abram reached Canaan but his father, Terah, never did. **Let us never forget that for everybody who makes it to Canaan, there is someone who doesn't.** For every Super Bowl hero, there are hundreds of young men who will never play in the NFL. For every movie star or musical artist, or famous person, there are millions of nameless faces that litter the landscape of "the almost." That's why some of us are so frustrated today. Despite all the promise and the potential, we have, we learned the hard way that sometimes talent and dreams, experience and desire, are not enough to get where you want to go.

However, there is a profound lesson hidden within Terah's story. When he traveled as far as Haran, he took his son Abram, grandson Lot, and daughter-in-law Sarai with him. This meant that when Abram later set out for Canaan, his journey was significantly shorter because his father had already covered part of the distance. This teaches us that even though we may not reach our own "Canaan," **what we do today, can pave the way for others to succeed tomorrow.**

To those who feel like they are not achieving their dreams, remember that your efforts are not in vain. What you do today, no matter how small it may seem, can have a profound impact on the future. Your journey, though incomplete, can shorten the path for others, allowing them to reach heights you could only imagine. So, let us continue to strive, knowing that our legacies are not just about our personal achievements but also about the opportunities we create for those who follow us. That's what the old people meant when they sang:

If I can help somebody, as I pass long,
If I can cheer somebody, with a word or song,
If I can show somebody, how they're traveling
wrong,
Then my living shall not be in vain.[16]

That's why you sacrifice for your kids. That's why you save and invest your money to leave a legacy for your children and your children's children. That's why you should stop doing some things and hanging out with some people. Your children are watching, and they only become what they see.

That's what Dr. King meant when he said these famous words, *"Like anybody, I would like to live a long life. Longevity has its place. But I'm not concerned about that now. I just want to do God's will. And he's allowed me to go up to the mountain. And I've looked over. And I've seen the Promised Land. I may not get there with you. But I want you to know tonight, that we, as a people, will get to the Promised Land!"*[17]

Once You Start Out for Canaan, Don't Stop

The story of Terah serves as a powerful metaphor for our own journeys. Why did he stop at Haran? Why did he settle? Theologians and historians speculate, but only he knows. Why did you stop? Why have you settled? Only you know. But one great lesson we learn from settling in Haran is: **once you start out for Canaan, don't stop.**

Why do we stop? Perhaps it's fear, grief, or the allure of comfort and familiarity. Whatever the reason, it's essential to remember that settling for mediocrity will never bring true satisfaction. The Bible doesn't reveal Terah's motivations, but it does show us that he never reached his intended destination.

Why should we keep going? Because once we start striving for excellence, pursuing our dreams, or living for a higher purpose, we must continue. Compromising our values or settling for less, can numb the pain temporarily but will ultimately leave us unfulfilled. Once you have a vision, or have established your goals, don't stop. Once you have set out for excellence, don't stop at mediocrity. Once you start living for God's glory, don't stop. Don't let the devil convince you to compromise who you are. I know it's calling you. I know it numbs the pain, but once you start out for recovery, don't stop. I know you are struggling. I know you are stressed out. I know you are worried about tomorrow. But once you start living for

God, don't stop. Keep praying. Keep standing on His word. Keep giving God the glory. For one thing I know about storms, if you keep the faith, there is deliverance, there is joy, there is hope, there is peace on the other side of through.

Hear me when I say this: **you can settle in Haran, but you will never be satisfied there.** That's why you should never stop. Don't stop for a husband or wife or friend or colleague. If they don't want no better, so be it. But don't you stop. Don't stop. Don't stop for your mother or father or sons or daughters. If they can't see themselves higher than they are, then leave them there. Don't stop! Don't listen to what the people say, for they may not see what you see, or feel what you feel, or know what you know.

Sometimes, amid your Haran, you must lay hands on your heart and say with conviction: "Don't stop, Charles. Don't measure your success based upon someone else's yardstick. What God has for me, is for me."

> **Actionable Steps:**
>
> **Reflect:** *Take time to reflect on your goals and aspirations.*
>
> **Realign:** *Ensure your actions align with your personal vision.*
>
> **Recommit:** *Reaffirm your commitment to your journey, no matter the obstacles.*
> *By embracing this mindset, you can break free from the limitations of external expectations and forge a path that truly reflects your potential. So, take a deep breath, stand tall, and remind yourself:*
>
> **"Don't stop. You are on a journey that is uniquely yours."**

The Bible says Abram made it to Canaan. But how? I ask. With all that he knew and all that he had to give up, what propelled him forward? What made him different from his Daddy? I submit to you that maybe the answer to this question is found in the opening verses of Genesis 12. The Bible says: *"Now the Lord said to Abram, 'Go from your country and your kindred and your father's house to the land that I will show you."*[18]

Perhaps that is the difference between Abram and his father. **Terah went to find Canaan, but**

Abram was sent there by God. Terah dreamed of Canaan, but Abram was sent there by God. Terah was his own pilot, but Abram was sent there by God. Terah was his own compass, his own GPS, but Abram was sent there by God.

We Went, vs. Being Sent

And perhaps that's the reason that Terah never made it to Canaan. **He went instead of being sent.** Don't misunderstand me, there is nothing wrong with having dreams and visions for your life. But before you set out on your journey, make sure that where you want to go is where God wants to send you. That's the reason that **some of us are having trouble in life and with our relationships. We went, instead of being sent.**

We went for Jessica Rabbit, when God was trying to send us a partner. We went for Big Pappa, when God was trying to send us Mr. Right. We went for the promotion and the raise, when God was trying to send us to our life's calling and our life's passion. We went for what we wanted, when God was trying to send us what we needed.

Let me see if I can say it this way: "If it feels good, let's do it." That's "a went" decision, "That's the way we have always done things." That's "a went" decision. "What's the easiest? What's the most convenient way?" That's "a went" decision. "What's popular? What's politically, correct?" That's "a went" decision. If all you care about is what feels good, smells good and looks good, that's "a went" decision. **But God told me to tell you, you will never get to Canaan with "a went" decision.**

Okay God, I hear you. So, how do I get to the Promised Land? **How do I get from "went" to "sent"?**

Proverbs 3:5-6 says: *"Trust in the Lord with all your heart and do not rely on your own insight. In all your ways acknowledge him, and he will make straight your paths."*

Proverbs 16:9 says: *"The human mind plans the way, but the Lord directs the steps."*

Matthew 7:7-8 says: *"Ask, and it will be given to you; search, and you will find: knock and the door will be opened for you. For everyone who asks receives, and everyone who searches finds, and for everyone who knocks, the door will be opened."*

Romans 12:2 says: *"Do not be conformed to this world, but be transformed by the renewing of your minds, so that you may discern what is the will of God – what is good and acceptable and perfect."*

But let me warn you: leaving Haran is no easy win. If you are vulnerable, there are temptations there. For Terah, Haran was rest from the journey. For Abram, Haran was security of the familiar. For Terah, Haran was progress from where he started. For Abram, Haran was living without growing. For Terah, Haran was more than he ever had. For Abram, Haran was progress without much sacrifice.

And if you are naïve, there are traps there. For they whisper in your ear: "It's okay that you settle in Haran. At least you are not where you started. It's okay that you settle in Haran. Maybe you don't need all that God has to offer. It's okay that you settle in Haran. Maybe the dream was too big. Maybe the vision was too audacious."

I don't know who I am talking to, but the devil is a liar! God told me to tell someone that **your days of settling in Haran are over.** Something BIG is getting ready to happen in your life. **Whatever you've been dreaming about, God is getting ready to create it. But don't miss this: you have to have something for God to work with.** If your mind is a blank canvas and you have no dreams, no hopes, no desires, no vision or your life, then this word is not for you. But if you are dreaming about something BIG, something greater than who you are right now, greater than anything you have ever accomplished, God is saying all I need you to do is go to where I'm sending you. Do what I am showing you. Believe what I am telling you.

Ladies and gentlemen, no matter what season of your life you are in, God is saying: "If you follow me, I will show you great and amazing things. If you follow me, I will show you visions that will dumbfound your naysayers. If you follow me, I will show you how to do some things that won't match your experience or your bank account."

When You Are Sent by God

God told Abram, "Go...and I will show you."[19]

That's what I love about God. **When God sends you, you have something that others who just went, don't have. YOU HAVE GOD'S PRESENCE.**

Isn't that your testimony, today? When we didn't know which way to go, we ended up going the wrong way, but somehow, we survived. God had to be with us. When we wanted to do wrong, but somehow, we ended up doing right. God had to be with us. When we took the foolish chances but somehow made it home anyhow. God had to be with us. When we went through the fire but didn't end up coming out smelling like smoke. God had to be with us. When we felt like giving up and we ended up going on anyhow. God had to be with us. When we had more than we could carry and ended up carrying it anyhow. Don't get it twisted; it was nobody but God with us.

God told Abram, *"I will make you a great nation, and I will bless you, and make your name great..."*[20]

Ladies and gentlemen, **when you are sent by God,** not only do you have God's presence, but you also **HAVE GOD'S PROVISIONS.** Folk may make you cry, but they can't conquer you. Folk may not like you, but they can't stop you. Folk may try to hurt your feelings, but they can't block your anointing. Folk may talk about you, but the Lord will send someone to talk for you.

When you are sent by God, little becomes much. Burdens turn into blessings. Problems become new possibilities. You might be saying, "I hear you, but I am still struggling with the initial question. Should I stay or should I go? How do I leave what I know? How do I know that there is something better for me? How do I know that Haran is not as good as it gets? How do I know that God will be there for me? How do I know that something BIG is getting ready to happen in my life? We know because God told Abram, ***"Go from your country..."***[21]

> *Don't miss this.* **The tense of the text is in the future tense.** *In other words, God is not telling Abram about what has happened, he's telling him what will happen. That's what happens* **when you are sent by God, you also have God's promise.**

When God sends you, you are not alone. You have God's presence, provision, and promise. This principle is evident in both biblical and historical contexts.

In the Bible:

- **Joseph:** Sold into slavery, Joseph rose to become a leader in Egypt, managing its resources during a famine. His success was not just due to his skills but also because he was guided by God's plan.[22]

- **Nehemiah:** He was called by God to rebuild Jerusalem's walls. Despite opposition, Nehemiah's faith and God's provision enabled him to complete the task, demonstrating how divine guidance can lead to remarkable achievements.[23]

In history:

- **Martin Luther King, Jr.:** A Baptist preacher who led the civil rights movement, King's faith was central to his mission. He believed that God was guiding him to fight for justice and equality, and his faith gave him the strength to persevere in the face of adversity.

- **Harriet Tubman:** An escaped slave who became a conductor on the Underground Railroad, Tubman credited her faith in God for her ability to lead hundreds to freedom. Her story shows how God's presence can empower individuals to achieve extraordinary feats.

In business:
- **David Green (Hobby Lobby):** Green built his company on Christian principles, ensuring that faith guided every business decision. His commitment to biblical values has led to both financial success and a positive impact on his community.

- **Mary Kay Ash:** Founder of Mary Kay Cosmetics, Ash attributed her success to her faith. She built a company culture based on the Golden Rule, empowering women and fostering a supportive environment that reflected her Christian values.

In each of these examples, the presence, provision, and promise of God were instrumental in achieving success. So, when faced with the question of whether to stay or go, remember God's promise is not just about what has happened but about what will happen. Trust in His guidance, and you will find that little becomes much, burdens turn into blessings, and problems become new possibilities. **GO!** With faith, knowing that God is with you every step of the way.

And as we stand at the threshold of our own "Haran," ready to embark on a journey towards our dreams, we have the promises of God. We have the promise that the same God who guided us through yesterday's challenges is the same God who will lead us into tomorrow's triumphs. We are fortified by the assurance that if God is for us, no one can stand against us[24]. We are shielded by the promise that no weapon formed against us will prosper[25]. We are comforted by the knowledge that every knee will bend, and every tongue will confess at the name of Jesus[26]. And we are sustained by the promise of eternal life, where heaven awaits us after this life is over.

These promises are not mere words; they are the foundations upon which we build our courage to leave our "Haran" behind. They remind us that our potential is limitless and that our dreams are within reach. Let us draw inspiration from the story of David, who faced the giant Goliath with unwavering faith in God's strength. Despite being told he was too young and inexperienced, David trusted that God would deliver him, just as He had from the lion and the bear[27]. And with a single stone, David defeated the giant, illustrating the power of faith and trust in God's promises.

In the business world consider the journey of Sara Blakely, the founder of Spanx. She faced numerous challenges in getting her product into stores, but instead of giving up, she took matters into her own hands. She went store to store, demonstrating her product and building a community around it. Her persistence paid off, and today Spanx is a household name.

Consider the story of Cindy Mi, the founder of VIPKid. Mi turned her passion for language into a successful online tutoring platform, connecting students from China with teachers in the U.S. and Canada. Despite initial challenges, she persevered and expanded her business into other courses, including Science, Math, and Coding.

And consider the story of Nelson Mandela as a testament to perseverance and faith. Mandela spent 27 years in prison for his activism against Apartheid but never lost sight of his vision for a free and equal South Africa. Upon his release, he became the first black president of South Africa, working tirelessly to dismantle apartheid and promote reconciliation.

52

God is Calling You to Take a Leap

Today, as you stand at your own crossroads, remember that **God is calling you to take the leap. GO!** Start that non-profit, open that business, write that book. Don't let fear or doubt hold you back. You are good enough, and you have what it takes. Don't let the voices of others discourage you; instead, let the promises of God be your guiding light. Something big is getting ready to happen in your life. Can you feel it? Can you see it? It's happening! It's happening! It's happening!

So, as you stand at your own crossroads, remember that God's call is not just about the destination but about the journey itself. It's about trusting in His plan and believing that He will make your name great, bless those who bless you, and curse those who curse you.[28]

In this moment of decision, let the courage of Abram inspire you. Take a deep breath, step out on faith, and watch as God unfolds a future filled with hope and promise. **GO!** With the assurance that God is with you every step of the way.

CHAPTER 3
Don't Give Up on Canaan

Genesis 11:31-12:5

31 *Terah took his son Abram and his grandson Lot son of Haran and his daughter-in-law Sarai, his son Abram's wife, and they went out together from Ur of the Chaldeans to go into the land of Canaan, but when they came to Haran, they settled there.* 32 *The days of Terah were two hundred five years, and Terah died in Haran.*

The Call of Abram

12 *Now the Lord said to Abram, "Go from your country and your kindred and your father's house to the land that I will show you.* 2 *I will make of you a great nation, and I will bless you and make your name great, so that you will be a blessing.* 3 *I will bless those who bless you, and the one who curses you I will curse, and in you all the families of the earth shall be blessed."* [a]

4 *So Abram went, as the Lord had told him, and Lot went with him. Abram was seventy-five years old when he departed from Haran.* 5 *Abram took his wife*

54

Sarai and his brother's son Lot and all the possessions that they had gathered and the persons whom they had acquired in Haran, and they set forth to go to the land of Canaan. When they had come to the land of Canaan, and they arrived there.

Let's be honest, parents. We love our children with every fiber of our being, but there are moments when they test our patience in ways we never thought possible. I'm not sure if this confession will earn me a halo or a spot in the parenting hall of shame, but I'm willing to risk it for the sake of authenticity. As a pastor, I've learned that sometimes the most sacred moments are the ones where we admit our imperfections and laugh together at the absurdities of life.

Take family road trips, for instance. You would think they would be a time for laughter, fellowship, joy and good old-fashioned family bonding. But let's face it, they often turn into a real-life remake of "National Lampoon's Vacation." It doesn't matter if we're at mile 10 or mile 150; inevitably, someone will utter those four dreaded words that every child seems to know and every parent dreads hearing: "Are we there yet?" Mile 5: "Are we there yet? Not yet, Max." Mile 100: "Are we there yet? Not yet, Skylar." Mile 30: "Are we there yet? Not yet, Madison." And by mile 400, all three of them are chiming in with the same annoying question, "Are we there yet?" To which I respond, with a mix of humor and exasperation, "Does this gas station look like Disney World to you?"

The Journey to Canaan: Are We There Yet?

Are we there yet? Isn't that the question your inner voice is asking you? When it comes to pursuing your dreams, whether it's going back to school, completing a business plan, finding a new job, or starting a new life, can you hear your aspirations asking your reality, *"Are we there yet?"* When it comes to forgiving past hurts, have you let go of the pain, the sorrow, the rejection? Or are you still holding on, stuck in a place where words remain just words and dreams are deferred? Are we there yet? Have we reached the point where our dreams are not just ideas but living realities? Are you still living off the faith of others: Nana's religion, Daddy's faith, Mama's prayers, or have you matured as a believer, knowing Jesus Christ for yourself? Are we there yet? How many times must God prove to us that if we are faithful to His word, He may not come when we want Him to, but He is still an on-time God?

The Bible tells us that Terah never made it to Canaan but died in Haran before reaching his final destination. Why did Terah settle? The Scriptures don't provide an answer, perhaps so we can see ourselves in his story. Was Terah like some of us, tired of the hardships that come with a long journey? Maybe he rationalized, "At least I made it to Haran. At least I made it farther than others did." Was Terah like some of us, a person who needed answers to his questions, a person who needed a sure thing, a person who needed to be in control? Could it be that since Terah worshipped idol gods in the land of Ur, he felt spiritually at home in Haran where they too worshipped the moon god? Or did Terah just resign himself to live up to the Hebrew translation of his name, which means a delay? Or was Terah one of those people who are pregnant with potential, but paralyzed by procrastination?

As we reflect on Terah's journey, let's ask ourselves: Are we settling for Haran when God has called us to Canaan? Are we allowing fear, doubt or complacency to hold us back from reaching our full potential? It's time to move forward, to trust in God's timing, and to believe that He is always working towards our good. Let's not let our dreams die in Haran. Let's press on toward Canaan, where our true destiny awaits.

Genesis 11:31-32 says: *31 Terah took his son Abram, his grandson Lot son of Haran, and his daughter-in-law Sarai, the wife of his son Abram, and together they set out from Ur of the Chaldeans to go to Canaan. But when they came to Haran, they settled there. 32 Terah lived 205 years, and died in Haran.*[29]

I don't know who needs to hear this: **don't die in a place called Haran without reaching your**

Promised Land. Regardless of what stage of life you are in or what success you may or may not have, it is critical for you to realize that **God is far more interested in your "finishing" than God is in your "starting."** Many have started out for Canaan, but they never completed the journey. Many have had potential, but they petered out. Many have had talent, but they never actualized it. Many were on the verge of something BIG but settled for less than what God wanted for them. The truth is some opportunities have an expiration date.

That's why you can't give up on Canaan. If God has given you a vision, walk in it. If God has given you a dream, receive it. If God has given you a purpose greater than you, don't get intimidated. Don't get scared. Embrace it. The writer of Hebrews reminds us: *"Let us hold fast to the confession of our hope without wavering, for he who has promised is faithful.30"*

Have you ever asked yourself, "Why am I in Haran?" **Maybe you are in Haran because God is repositioning you in a controlled environment.** Haran was never to be Terah's final destination. It was just a transition point on the journey that God was taking him. A safe place where you try different things, you grow in different ways. Haran was supposed to be the place where you could experiment and fail and fail again, each time getting wiser, each time getting stronger. Haran was supposed to be the place where you could confront your fears because by confronting your fears, they could no longer be your limits.

Haran was supposed to be the place where you could dream big, for if your dreams don't scare you, they are not big enough. Haran was supposed to be the place where you gained experience and wisdom because experience is learning something every day and wisdom is letting something go every day. Haran was supposed to be the place of transformation and change because you can't find your purpose until you go process. Haran was supposed to be the place where you learn that growth is uncomfortable and messy and full of feelings you were not expecting. Haran was supposed to be the place where your faith was stretched and matured so when the valleys come you won't give up and when the mountains appear you won't stop climbing.

That's why some of you are in Haran. It's not punishment. It's not the end of the story. It's just God's way of getting you ready for the big things he has in store for you.

You thought losing your job was the end of you. But God was just trying to take something out of your life in order to put something greater in it. You thought when he walked out on you and left you with the kids that your life was over. But God was just trying to show you that you don't need a man to make you whole. You are stronger than you really know. You thought cancer and diabetes and mental illness and HIV were death sentences. But God was just giving you a testimony that life is not defined by a doctor's report. **Life is defined by the life we live and the legacy we leave.**

Why am I in Haran? **Maybe you are in Haran because the vision is right, but you are not ready.** What do you mean by that, Pastor? Yes, God is great and yes, God is good and there is nothing that God cannot do. But there are moments in life that we have to practice "patient, impatience." What's patient impatience, you ask? Is it, "what will be, will be?" No, that's passive resignation. Is it, "I'm just going to sit here and wait on God?" No, that's complacency. Is it, "This is just what it is?" No, that's fatalism. Is it, "I'm just going to suck it up and bear it?" No, that's defeat. Patient impatience is active waiting. It's about being prepared, working towards your goals, and trusting in God's timing.

I'm reminded of the making of a pearl. One of the most annoying things that can ever happen to an oyster is to have lodged within its shell a tiny grain of sand. Most of the time when this happens, the oyster is able to locate the grain of sand and expel it from its shell. In fact, the oyster finds the grain of sand, removes it and the oyster is all good. Yet, there are those rare occasions, maybe 1 out of 100 times, that the oyster just can't seem to do it. It works and works, and tries and tries, yet despite all its energy, and its might and its efforts to expel the grain of sand, it just can't. So, the oyster becomes irritated and frustrated and exacerbated because it finds itself in a situation, or a circumstance that is beyond its control. Yet, what the oyster does next is fascinating to me. The oyster says: "Since I can't get rid of the sand, let me embrace it."

So, the oyster secretes a fluid to coat the irritant. Layer upon layer of this coating is deposited on the irritant until the sand is transformed into a beautiful pearl. I don't know who needs to hear this: a pearl is a beautiful thing that is produced by a frustrated life. If there was no frustration, if there was no problem, if there was no irritant, if there was no patience, there would be no pearl. **Sometimes our blessings are born in the crucible of frustration, because the proof of our faith is not change, it's patience.**

The Proof of Our Faith Is Not Change. It's Patience.

Here lies the problem. We love the pearls, but we don't love the process. Yet, there is something you need to learn about God: **You don't get to God's blessings without active waiting.** Ask yourself this question, "Have I done everything I can do, to walk in the vision that God has for my life?" The amazing thing about God is that at any given moment, God can send the increase. At any given moment, God can send the healing. At any given moment, God can send the deliverance. But don't miss the point. Our job is not to open the door. Our job is to be ready when the door opens.

Genesis 11:31 says, *"Terah took his son Abram and his grandson Lot son of Haran, and his daughter-in-law Sarai, his son Abram's wife, and they went out together from Ur of the Chaldeans to go into the land of Canaan;* **but when they came to Haran, they settled there.***"*

Despite the vision, despite the provision, despite covering, Terah settles in Haran. **That's what sometimes happens with dreams. You get the vision, but you also get the doubt.**

I remember the time my oldest daughter ran track for the first time. To her surprise, and to the surprise of others around her, she broke the middle school regional and school record for the triple jump. Coming into this year, she was no longer the unknown girl on the team, she was the star. She was the only middle school student asked by the head coach to work out with the varsity team. Her coaches and classmates alike were projecting that Madison would smash other records and establish herself as one of the best track athletes that Lovett ever had. They could see it. She could see it. But that was before she got beat in the triple jump the next meet. And not only did she get beat, but the girl broke her school record. I was there. I could feel her pain. I could see the disappointment in her face. I could hear the hurt and the doubt in her voice. And that's how life is sometimes when the vision comes, the doubt comes as well. I can still hear her saying to me, "Daddy, she beat me. Maybe I'm not as good as I think I am. Maybe I'm not as good as they say I am."

Yet, an hour later I got a text from Madison that simply said: "Daddy, I know I can beat her. I know I can jump farther. I know I can run faster. When Spring Break comes, instead of hanging out with my friends, I'm going to focus on my diet and work on my technique and work on my conditioning. You will see. When I come back after the break, I'll be ready to win."

That's what you must do when the doubt comes and your confidence wanes. You must lay hands on yourself and declare, "Yes, I can." That's what Senator Barak Obama did in 2007. When the political pundits said he was too young. When the haters said the Clinton machine was too powerful. When the folk who looked like him said the country wasn't ready. He simply looked through the lens of hope and declared, "Yes, we can." I believe there is someone reading this book who needs to say those words over your life: "Yes, I can." Yes, I can triumph over heartache and heartbreak. Yes, I can rise above loneliness and brokenness. Yes, I can conquer and rise above obesity and disease. Yes, I can prevail over squandered moments and missed opportunities. The Apostle Paul is right when he says, *"I can do all things through Christ that strengthens me."*[31]

Maybe that's what separated Abram from his father. He had the faith his father never had. Hebrews 11:8 says: *"By faith, Abraham obeyed when he was called to set out for a place that he was to receive as an inheritance; and he set out, not knowing where he was going."*

Reaching Canaan can be a daunting task, but no matter what the world says, we must never underestimate what we can do. **When we limit God to our circumstances, we cancel out our faith and throw away our hope.** That's what Hebrews 11:1 really means: *"Faith is the substance of the things hoped for, the evidence of things not seen."* Too often, we misinterpret the text by thinking faith is the star of the text, when hope is really the star. Hope is what keeps us pushing, grinding, striving, working, growing, producing, thriving and dreaming.

Somebody recently asked me, "Why do people give up on their dreams?" To which I simply responded, "Without hope, faith has no job." That's why some of us are where we are. We lost our hope and settled for Haran when Canaan has been promised to us.

I remember a moment in my life when I stood at a crossroads, torn between two worlds. On one hand, the corporate world beckoned with promotions and opportunities, validating years of hard work and sacrifice. But God had given me a vision of planting a church called the Breakthrough Fellowship. And to His glory, the vision was blooming.

That's why I was so excited when I was invited to attend a conference with 200 of the most influential and successful pastors in the Black church community. In my mind, I said to myself, "I'm out of my league. I'm not in their weight class. I'm not worthy of being in the room. These men had more people watching them on the internet than we had in our whole church." But I was there. I was in the number. I was in the room.

As fate would have it, my euphoria was short-lived. I received a phone call from the COO of my corporation. He said, "Charles, out of hundreds of possible candidates, you have made it to the final round of interviews. This interview will determine if you become the next CEO of this division. Make plans to come to New York City in the next two weeks. I look forward to seeing you."

You must understand that this is a position I have coveted my whole career. This was a position 20 years in the making. This position meant more money, more power, national recognition, and exposure. This position wasn't just a change in title. This position could change the trajectory of my family's financial future forever. It meant international travel. It meant leading a multimillion-dollar business and being responsible for people around the world. This was the job I've been working so hard and so long for. Yet, when I hung up the phone, instead of being excited, tears began running down my face. I asked God, "Why this opportunity and why now? I thought you told me to launch a local church. I thought you told me to concentrate on my ministry. How can I do this job and be a father, a husband, and a pastor? There's no way. The job is too big. The demands are too great."

As I stood there, feeling the weight of the decision, God spoke to me through the Holy Spirit: "Do you know why you are here in Arizona? Do you know why you are in this room with these great pastors? Do you know why your COO personally called you about this opportunity?" I must admit, I sheepishly said, "No. I don't know why I'm here. I don't know why I got this call." And the Holy Spirit clearly spoke to me these words, **"You got the call because I wanted to give you a glimpse of what you could do. And you are here because I wanted to show you where I can take you."**

Don't mistake Haran for Canaan

I don't know who needs to hear this word but **don't mistake Haran for Canaan.** What you can see is Haran. What God can show you is Canaan. What you can do is Haran. What God can do is Canaan. The resources you have is Haran. The resources God can give you is Canaan. Sometimes, God must get us in a place where you can clearly hear him say: *"There are some places you can get to, but there are some places only I can show you."*

The Bible says, now the Lord said to Abram, *"Go to the land I will show you."* And the writer of Genesis records that Abram went as the Lord told him. As I interviewed for the job, I didn't know if it was God's will for me to get the job. I didn't know how big my church would be. I didn't know what the history books would ultimately record about my ministry. And I didn't know, if God blessed me with everything, how I would balance it all. But one thing I did know: **the life that God had for me, was larger than the life I was living.**

The Life God Has for You

That's my encouragement to you. **The life that God has for you is often larger than the life you are living.** That's what Abram discovered. Despite his age, despite his circumstances, despite the people around him and the things he had to leave behind, Abram went as the Lord told him. And the Bible says God kept his promise. He made Abram's name great. God blessed him and made him a blessing to others. And in time, God showed him the Promised Land.

I don't know your story, but the Lord told me to tell you: **don't give up on Canaan.** This is the moment that God is going to allow you to take your dreams by the hand. This is the year you are going to be able to reach out and touch the things you thought were never going to happen in your life. I know the devil is trying to convince you to throw in the towel and to die in Haran, but there's no limit to what God can do.

So, I ask you today: Are you ready to step into the unknown? Are you ready to trust in the power of God? Are you ready to believe that God can do the impossible? Are you ready to see the Promised Land of your dreams? Because I tell you, it's not just a promise. It's a reality waiting to unfold.

Don't let fear hold you back. Don't let doubt whisper lies in your ear. You are on the cusp of a miracle. You are on the edge of a breakthrough. And when you take that first step of faith, when you refuse to give up on Canaan, you will discover that God is not just with you, God is ahead of you, preparing the way for your greatness. He is clearing the path, removing obstacles, and illuminating your journey. Your destiny is calling, and it's time to answer.

CHAPTER 4
Don't Let the Noise Stop You

Genesis 11:25-12:7

25 and Nahor lived after the birth of Terah one hundred nineteen years and had other sons and daughters.

26 When Terah had lived seventy years, he became the father of Abram, Nahor, and Haran.

Descendants of Terah

27 Now these are the descendants of Terah. Terah was the father of Abram, Nahor, and Haran, and Haran was the father of Lot. 28 Haran died before his father Terah in the land of his birth, in Ur of the Chaldeans. 29 Abram and Nahor took wives; the name of Abram's wife was Sarai, and the name of Nahor's wife was Milcah. She was the daughter of Haran the father of Milcah and Iscah. 30 Now Sarai was barren; she had no child.

31 Terah took his son Abram and his grandson Lot son of Haran and his daughter-in-law Sarai, his son Abram's wife, and they went out together from Ur of the Chaldeans to go into the land of Canaan, but when

they came to Haran, they settled there. 32 The days of Terah were two hundred five years, and Terah died in Haran.

The Call of Abram

12 Now the lord said to Abram, "Go from your country and your kindred and your father's house to the land that I will show you. 2 I will make of you a great nation, and I will bless you and make your name great, so that you will be a blessing. 3 I will bless those who bless you, and the one who curses you I will curse, and in you all the families of the earth shall be blessed."[a]

4 So Abram went, as the lord had told him, and Lot went with him. Abram was seventy-five years old when he departed from Haran. 5 Abram took his wife Sarai and his brother's son Lot and all the possessions that they had gathered and the persons whom they had acquired in Haran, and they set forth to go to the land of Canaan. When they had come to the land of Canaan, 6 Abram passed through the land to the place at Shechem, to the oak[b] of Moreh. At that time the Canaanites were in the land. 7 Then the Lord appeared to Abram and said, "To your offspring I will give this land." So, he built there an altar to the Lord, who appeared to him.

In today's world, opinions are as abundant as the air we breathe. Turn on the TV, and you're bombarded by pundits from every corner of the political spectrum, each convinced they hold the truth. Scroll through social media, and you'll find a cacophony of voices, each one louder than the last, sharing their thoughts on everything from politics to pop culture. Even at the local barber shop, debates rage on about who's the greatest athlete of all time, with each participant convinced their opinion is the only one that matters.

But let's be honest: opinions are a dime a dozen. Everybody has one. Celebrities and unknowns alike have become self-proclaimed authorities, sharing their views on everything under the sun. Yet, amidst this sea of opinions, there's one voice that stands out: the voice of God.

When I read about God's call and promise to Abram in Genesis 11:31-12:2, it stopped me in my tracks. Here was a man who wasn't just following his own dreams or opinions but was being sent by God on a journey that would change history. This story raises critical questions: What does it mean to be called by God? How do we distinguish his voice from the noise of the world? And what happens when we choose to follow his plan, instead of our own?

In a world where everyone has an opinion, Abram's story reminds us that there's a difference between following our own desires and being sent by God. So, let's take a moment to listen beyond the noise of the world and hear the voice that truly matters. **What is God saying to you today?**

In chapter 11, we see God bring His focus down from all of mankind to the family of Terah. You may recall that back in Genesis chapter 2, God moved us from an overview of creation to the account of man by rotating his telephoto lens from wide angle to zoom. In chapter 1 of Genesis, the focus is on all creation. In chapter 2, the focus zooms in to record the creation of humanity. Several generations removed and hundreds of years later, Terah was born. When we meet Terah in our text, he was living in the city of Ur with his three sons, Abram, Nahor and Haran. Haran died. Sometime later, we don't know how much later, Terah took Abram and his wife Sarai and Lot, the son of Haran who had died, and the Bible says, *they set out from Ur of the Chaldeans to go to Canaan."* We don't know why Terah wanted to leave Ur. It could have been because of a desire to get away from the idolatry which permeated the city of Ur, for Ur was a center of moon worship. It could have been that he left over his grief for Haran. It could have been that God called him to go. We don't know. What we do know is that Terah never made it to Canaan. He wanted to go. He started in that direction. But the Bible says, in Genesis 11:31, *"But when they came to Haran, they settled there."* The Hebrew word for "settled" means "to sit down." Terah put his roots down in Haran, and there, according to Genesis 11:32, Terah died.

The simple suggestion of this story is that Terah had a dream to make it to Canaan, but the dream died with him in Haran. That still happens today. Most people, at one time or another, have a dream, a dream of what they want to do or who they want to be or where they want to go. But instead of making it to the Canaan of their dreams, many people die with their dream in Haran.

As I came to chapter 12, I wondered how Abram's friends responded when he told them that he had a dream that he was leaving the comfort and the familiarity of Haran to go to a land that God wouldn't even tell him the name. I wondered if they said, "That's what your daddy said, but look at him."

I wondered what the people on the job thought when he handed in his resignation and told his boss the money was right, but the job didn't satisfy his soul. I wondered what his people said when he told them he was packing light because God said, "**everybody that was for him, couldn't go with him.**" I wondered how fast the gossip spread when social media got word that Abram, with his barren wife and his tag-along nephew, were setting out on a new adventure. "Sister did you hear the news? Old man Abram has lost his mind. Viagra may work but Sarai can't have any kids." "Brother, can you believe Abram quit his good job? The word on the street is...he walked away from his pension and his 401k Plan...all for a dream. Didn't he fail at this before? Doesn't he know he's too old for this foolishness? Dreams and visions are a young man's games."

Everybody has an opinion. That's why I come with a word for that person God is calling to their destiny. Whatever you do, no matter what the peanut gallery says, **don't let the noise stop you.** You may not know how, you may not know when, but something BIG is getting ready to happen in your life.

> *There will always be some kind of noise that will try to throw you off rhythm and distractions that are designed to drown out your focus and disrupt your flow. Yet, when you keep your ear tuned to God's voice, even in the chaos of the noise makers, God will give you the clarity to move forward with confidence.*

The Noise Makers

There are the **DREAM KILLERS.** They are the nay sayers, the haters and the doubters that talk behind your back and smile in your face.[32] They are the ones with small talk and small minds. They are the ones who question your skills and doubt your intellect. They are the crabs in the basket. If they can't get out, nobody can get out. They are the ones that say: *"Don't you know that you don't have the experience? Don't you know that you don't have the pedigree? Don't you know that* *other folk have tried before with no success? What makes you so special?"*

Dream killers are on your job. Dream killers are in your family. Dream killers are in the church. Dream killers are all around you. But despite the noise, remember that sometimes prophecy is in your haters' mouths. How could this be, you ask? **You will never know your greatness until you see how much your haters try to block you.**

Someone once asked me: "How do you now if something big is happening in your life?" I simply replied to them, "Listen to the chatter." That's the reason why your haters hate you. That's the reason why the opposition is so fierce. That's the reason why all the naysayers are trying to block your flow. They see the anointing in your life. They see the potential within you. They see the power all around you. The Adversary is not naïve. The Adversary knows that BIG things often come from small beginnings. The Adversary isn't fighting you over where you are. The Adversary is fighting you over where you are going. Yet can I encourage you? Don't let the noise stop you.

Then there are **THE ENABLERS.** They are the people who cosign your mediocrity. They are the people who say it's okay that you don't try again. They preach practicality over passion, security over sacrifice. They are the people who say passion and dreams are overrated. You have responsibilities. You have obligations. They are the people who remind us that average is good and settling is okay. Because they say, don't be foolish. You have responsibilities. You have obligations. They are the people who say it's okay that you don't love him, at least you have a man. It's okay that you settle for her, it's better than being without.

Yet can I say this to you? **You can't be who you were and who you are at the same time.** You can't be mediocre and be a visionary. You can't be a settler and a dreamer. You can't think small thoughts and do big things. At some point, you must let go of this kind of schizophrenic personality and lay claim to the promise that God has for you.

Lay hands on yourself and say this with me: *"Greatness is all over me." Say it again. This time, say it like you really mean it: "Greatness is all over me."*

Today I need you to be your own life coach and declare with your lips: *"I might have been complacent and lacked motivation and have gone through life with blinders on. But that was then; this is now. Since I have found Jesus, I know I am valuable. I know I'm beautifully made. I know I'm extraordinary in every way. I know I am good enough."*

Jesus didn't shed his blood on Calvary for us to live lives of mediocrity and complacency. I don't care what the world says, you have greatness all over you. It might be buried underneath some stuff right now, but rest assured, God is getting ready to do a new thing in your life.

Then there is **THE ESTABLISHMENT.** They are the ones that remind you, "That's not how we do things around here. That's not how you worship. That's not how you do church. That's not our protocol." That's why there is so much noise around you. Because **whenever you don't fit the culture, the culture will become critical of you.**

You must understand that whenever you attempt to bring about change, it invokes the insecurities of those who have become accustomed to the way things have always been. In some respects, new visions are often seen as threats. What "should be" will be perceived by others as the very thing that "should not be." And to make matters worse, the establishment is often armed with facts. History and experience are on their side; a vision is about the future and not the past. And yet, history and experience are often the very ingredients that give birth to a vision.

The Bible says Sarai was barren. So how could God make Abram a great nation? His father Terah settled in Haran and died there. So how could Abram leave what he knew? God's promise couldn't be verified. So, how could he risk starting over again? It didn't compute. It didn't make logical sense. But that's how life is. There comes a point in all our lives that the noise will become so loud in our ears that it will convince us that what we are dreaming is crazy. Yet, it is in those crazy moments that God does God's best work.

I remember when my oldest daughter Madison was born. My wife, Jennifer, was in labor for 3 days. The pain was intense. The moment was tense. I remember the worry on the doctor's and nurses' faces. The baby couldn't come out. The more Jennifer pushed, the more Madison got stuck. I remember the nurse getting on the table and pushing on Jennifer's stomach. And I remember how she screamed out in pain. But thanks be to God, Madison was born fine and healthy. I must admit, at that moment, Jennifer and I both thought that Madison would be the only child we would have. The pain was too much. The drama was too extreme. But after the pain subsided, the desire to try again returned.

That's how it is with a God-given vision. It won't always compute. It won't always make logical sense. But every time you put your dreams to rest, God will send you another word, a greater passion to try again. Sometimes when it comes to your dreams, you must be stubborn about it and ask yourself, why not? Owning my own home? Why not? Breaking my addictions? Why not? Being whole again? Why not? Rebuilding after a set-back? Why not? Overcoming the shame of abuse and neglect? Why not? Being happy in who I am? Why not? Having the courage to be vulnerable again? Why not? Following your passions and achieving your dreams? Why not?

Verse 1 says: *"Now the Lord said to Abram, "Go from your country and your kindred and your father's house to the land that I will show you."* Now look at verse 7: *"Then the Lord appeared to Abram and said, "To your offspring I will give this land."*

Look closely at the text. The promise to give the land to Abram that is found in verse 7 is preceded by God's promise to show him the land in verse 1. In other words, "show" becomes "give" when Abram makes his move. I don't know who needs this word, but you need to know that **God has something BIG to give you but first, you must make a move**.

Go after your dreams. Go after your dreams. Go after your dreams. That's my word for you when the noise comes. When other people give up, keep dreaming. When other people are sleeping, keep working. When other people play the blame game, don't let yourself fall into the trap. Instead, look within yourself and keep doing the small things that make the big things come true. And when other people are laughing at your progress, don't let the noise stop you. The Bible says that when God called Abram, he didn't give him all the answers. He told him WHAT, he told him WHERE, but he didn't tell him HOW.

How? That's the question some of us are wrestling with. With the experience I have, HOW am I going to get this ministry off the ground? With their Daddy gone, HOW am I going to protect my children and make the ends meet? With the debts that we have,

HOW are we ever going to tithe and be debt free? With Mama gone, HOW am I going to keep on living? With all your broken promises, HOW are we going to put this marriage back together again? HOW? HOW are we going to survive? That's the nature of visions. **Visions usually come with blind spots.**

Visions Usually Come with Blind Spots

In biology, the blind spot is where the optic nerve and blood vessels leave the eyeball. Each of our eyes has a tiny functional blind spot about the size of a pinhead. In this tiny area, where the optic nerve passes through the surface of the retina, there are no photoreceptors. Since there are no photoreceptor cells detecting light, it creates a bind spot. Without photoreceptor cells, the eye cannot send any messages about the image to the brain, which usually interprets the image for us. You're likely not even aware of your blind spot in day-to-day living, because your brain fills in any missing information.

In driving, blind spots are areas or zones on the road that cannot be seen by a driver while looking at rearview or side mirrors. However, in life, blind spots are the areas in our life that we refuse to change or the areas that we refuse to allow our faith to touch, Vengeance and anger create blind spots. Fear and low self-esteem create blind spots. Stagnation and complacency create blind spots.

Yet, vision also comes with blind spots. Growth and progress come with blind spots. Change and transformation come with blind spots. New beginnings and new levels come with blind spots. Yet, the good news of the Gospel is, visions might come with blind spots for us, but they never create blind spots for God.

When God gave the vision for our church that we call The Breakthrough Fellowship, I was so excited about what God had done. With no money and with no "mother church" and with no celebrity, my wife and I started a Bible study in our house that grew into a ministry. From a Bible study to a new local church in a movie theater to the growing church that we are today, the church and I experienced the supernatural favor of God through the years. Yet, I must admit, the vision came with blind spots.

While my wife and I grew up as preachers' children, neither one of us had pastored before. Even though I served on the ministerial staff of great pastors and modeled my ministry after my father and father-in-law, I wasn't prepared for the challenges that come with the title Senior pastor. The Breakthrough Fellowship is my first and only church that I have pastored and while the vision and the calling that God has given me has never dimmed, I must admit the noise of my fears and the blind spots of my mistakes have left me with moments of questioning my call and doubting my gifts. Despite the success achieved and the lives God has blessed us to touch, I haven't been deaf to the whispers or the complaints or the laughs of my critics, or blind to the people who no longer call our church home.

Yet, I'm reminded of what God said to Abram in chapter 12. I didn't call you to be perfect. I called you to be obedient. God said to Abram and the Holy Spirit is saying to you and me: **God knows your blind spots and your shortcomings and your faults and failures. Yet, God also knows your gifts, and your heart, and the anointing on your life.** Therefore, no matter how loud the noise becomes within and around your head, if you are obedient to the call and the vision of God, despite the blind spots you will and may have, God will show you. God will lead you. God will coach you. God will navigate you because **God will never give you a vision without also giving you a plan.**

God Never Gives Vision Without a Plan

When God called Abram, God had a plan. God knew HOW He was going to make his name great. God knew HOW He was going to bless him. God knew HOW He was going to cover him. God knew HOW He was going to protect him. God knew HOW He was going to promote him.

And that's how it is for you. God has a plan for your life. Many times, visions die in the time between WHAT and HOW. What makes you so special? What makes you so unique? What makes this attempt different from the last failed one?

I don't know about you, but sometimes it's just easier for me to lower my sights, let go of the vision and shoot for a target I know I have some hopes of hitting. But my good news for you today is simply this: **God specializes in the HOW.** God knows HOW you are going to get this ministry off the ground. God knows HOW you are going to protect your children even though their Daddy is gone. God knows HOW to make the ends meet. God knows HOW to bring restoration and joy back into your life. God knows HOW to heal your body. God knows HOW to put your marriage back together again. God knows how to defeat the giants you will face. God knows how to climb over the obstacles in front of you. God knows how to navigate through troubled waters in your life.

Whatever they said about you or to you, God is saying: "Don't let noise stop you. I know how to cancel it." Abram, I know your Daddy settled for less but go to the land that I will show you. Abram, I know you have some false starts and some setbacks on your resume but go to the land that I will show you. Abram, I know what they are saying about you but go to the land that I will show you. Abram, I know the noise distracted you for a minute but go to the land that I will show you.

And beloved, that's the shout[33] found in the text. Abram listened to God over the noise in his head and all around him. The Bible says, "Abram went, as the Lord had told him..." Sight unseen, Abram went as the Lord told him. With more questions than answers, Abram went as the Lord told him. With a WHAT and WHERE but without a HOW, Abram went as the Lord told him.

That's how you conquer the noise swarming around your head, you keep your mind stayed on Jesus. **Because a God-given vision isn't predicated on logic. It's rooted in faith.** The Bible says Abram's Daddy died. His wife was barren. He had to leave what he knew. But through it all, verse 7 says, he worshipped God anyhow.

I'm about to confuse the Adversary right now. The Adversary thinks you can only praise God when things are going well but the sign of a true worshipper is that a true worshipper can give God glory even when they are having a bad day. Where are the worshippers in the house? If you know God is true, if you know God is good in the good times and in the bad times, I dare you to open your mouth and give God glory!

One of the great films of 1999 was The Matrix starring Keanu Reeves. It's a futuristic sci-fi movie, where the world has been taken over by computers. The computers need the energy that comes from human bodies, so they keep a supply of genetically engineered humans in a permanently anaesthetized state. They then create an imaginary world for the comatose humans, The Matrix, in which people think themselves alive and conscious, going to work, living normal everyday lives. The Matrix is the world that has been literally over everyone's eyes to blind them from the truth, a world that keeps them in bondage and acceptance of the way things are. But there is a group of rebels who have broken free of the Matrix. Led by Morpheus, they lead a shadow life committed to an alternate reality and hunted by cyber cops. Then they discover a character, Neo, (Keanu Reeves) the prophesied One who will break people free from the Matrix.

Early in the film we find Neo awakening to the truth. During part of the Matrix, the computer created illusion, he experiences unexplainable doubts about the way things are, doubts which act like a splinter in his mind, making him feel uncomfortable. Then he is introduced to the rebels, led by Morpheus. Morpheus offers Neo a chance to see the truth. He holds out two pills. The blue pill is a pleasant analgesic which will blur over the pain his honest enquiry is creating. Swallow the blue pill and he'll be comfortably back in the Matrix. Or he can take the red pill, which will open his eyes to see new possibilities, to carve out a place in the alternate reality.

Friends, at the heart of the Gospel is the idea that we are caught in the Matrix, in a false reality that presupposes that without a Savior we are destined to live a life of mediocrity, sin and brokenness. Yet, God so loved the world that Jesus came so that whoever believes in Him shall not only have life but have it more abundantly.

The Bible says Abram went as the Lord had told him and without opening his mouth, Abram declared, *"I believe God."* That's the mindset you need to have to claim the destiny God has shown you. When the noise starts, when opposition comes, when the doubts rise, when the blind spots occur, when the culture is critical, when you have a what and you don't know the how, remember Abram and declare by faith: ***I believe God.***

I believe God. *If I'm faithful over a few things, God will put me in charge of many.34*

I believe God. *What the enemy meant to kill me, God will use it for my good.35*

I believe God. *They who wait on the Lord shall renew their strength.36*

I believe God. *Weeping may endure for a night, but joy comes in the morning.37*

I believe God. *The Lord is my shepherd; I shall not want.38*

I believe God*. Even though I walk through the valley of the shadow of death, I shall fear no evil.39*

I believe God. Jesus loves me. Jesus can redeem me. Jesus died for me and one day He is coming back again.

Others might not understand, and others might not see what you see. Yet, when the noise gets loud, don't let it stop you. Instead, encourage yourself with the words spoken by Abram, ***"I believe God!"***

CHAPTER 5
What if your Dreams are Waiting on You?

Acts 7:2-5
2 And Stephen replied: "Brothers[a] and fathers, listen to me. The God of glory appeared to our ancestor Abraham when he was in Mesopotamia, before he lived in Haran, 3 and said to him, 'Leave your country and your relatives and go to the land that I will show you.' 4 Then he left the country of the Chaldeans and settled in Haran. After his father died, God had him move from there to this country in which you are now living. 5 He did not give him any of it as a heritage, not even a foot's length, but promised to give it to him as his possession and to his descendants after him, even though he had no child.

Genesis 12:1-4
The Call of Abram
12 Now the Lord said to Abram, "Go from your country and your kindred and your father's house to the land that I will show you. 2 I will make of you a great nation, and I will bless you and make your name

great, so that you will be a blessing. ³ *I will bless those who bless you, and the one who curses you I will curse, and in you all the families of the earth shall be blessed."[a]*

⁴ *So Abram went, as the Lord had told him, and Lot went with him. Abram was seventy-five years old when he departed from Haran.*

What if your dreams are waiting for you? Not lost, not forgotten, not impossible, simply waiting. Waiting for you to notice them. Waiting for you to believe in them again. Waiting for you to take that first courageous step.

What if God is calling us to live beyond ourselves: to feed the hungry, to speak truth to power, give to the needy, to lead someone to Jesus Christ, and to change the world? What if God's visions for our lives are more than just eating, sleeping, working, and paying taxes? What if, in the midst of all the madness that marks some of our pasts, the history books will record that God was just preparing us for something BIG that is getting ready to happen in our lives? What if, despite our sins and transgressions, despite our fears and failures, God's greatest vision for our lives is for us to give ourselves permission to dream again?

Dreams...we all have them. As children, we dreamed of becoming doctors, astronauts, preachers, teachers, moms, and dads. As children, we dreamed of our wedding day, of throwing the winning touchdown, of performing in front of thousands, of seeing our name up in lights. Then something happened. Somewhere, in the process of growing up, we quit dreaming. Safety and security took the place of risk and adventure. Living and bills took the place of hopes and dreams. Reality and cynicism took the place of miracles and wonders.

But what if? What if our heart's desires were planted there by God himself? What if our dreams are not just fantasies, but a blueprint for our destiny? What if we are meant to live a life that is bigger than we ever imagined?

The Acts of the Apostles Chapter 7 verses 2-4 records these words: *"And Stephen replied: Brothers and fathers listen to me. The God of glory appears to our ancestor Abraham when he was in Mesopotamia, before he lived in Haran, 3 and said to him, 'Leave your country and your relatives and go to the land that I will show you.' 4 Then he left the country of the Chaldeans and settled in Haran. After his father died, God had him move from there to this country in which you are now living."*

By Stephen's account, God came to Abram in a dream while they were in Ur and gave him a vision to leave the familiar and the safety and security of his homeland. God promised Abram and his descendants that He would be his God, his protector, his sustainer and his strong tower[40]. The one and true God promised Abram that he would use him as an instrument to bless the whole world, and that Abram's new home would be in Canaan. But when we turn to Genesis 11, we discover that Abram, still hadn't made it to Canaan.

He had dreams but life happened. He had dreams but his Daddy died. He had dreams but his wife couldn't get pregnant. He had dreams but he was an older man now. He had dreams but he had bills to pay. He had dreams but he had folk to support. He had dreams but this is what he knew. And like Abram, you had dreams too. You had dreams, but that was before the divorce. You had dreams, but that was before the doctor's report. You had dreams, but that was before the pink slip. You had dreams, but that was before your innocence was taken. You had dreams, but that was before you got pregnant. That was before he put hands on me. That was before the bankruptcy, before the prognosis, before the failure, before the set-back.

And like Abram, some of us find ourselves in Haran with a dream deferred. Yet hear me when I say this: don't get comfortable where you are. Where you are isn't where you are supposed to be. God has something bigger for you. God has something better for you. Despite his complacency, despite his circumstances, despite his aborted dreams, God appears to Abram again and says, "**I dare you to dream again.**"

Dreams Becoming Reality: Now!

I'm in Genesis Chapter 12 now. The word says, "***Now the Lord said to Abram...***"

Before you read that interjection too quickly, don't miss what God is saying to us about our dreams. **The process of our dreams becoming a reality starts NOW.** Not tomorrow, not in two days but NOW. Not when you get yourself together, or when things are simple, but NOW. Not when it makes sense to you, or you can see your way to the finish line, but NOW. Not when there are no problems, or when all the bills are paid, but NOW.

Not after you make every excuse about why you can't, or procrastinate through another year, but NOW. Not after you seek permission from people who have no authority over your future or wait for someone to validate what God has already anointed, but NOW. Not after you berate yourself for past mistakes or past failures or dreams deferred, but NOW. Not when folk agree, not when you know the outcome on the other side of through, but NOW.

God is saying to us: I need you to surrender to me NOW. I need you to follow me NOW. I need you to believe what I showed you NOW. I need you to step out on faith NOW. I know your history. I know your background. I know your pedigree. I know what you are working with. I'm not worried about any of those things. I just need you to dream again NOW.

Genesis 12:1 says: *"Now the Lord said to Abram, "Go from your country and your kindred and your father's house to the land that I will show you."*

Don't miss this. Not only is God saying to us, now is the time to activate your faith and to realize your dreams. God is also saying: **GO even when you don't have all the answers.**

The real tests of your faith are not the things you hold onto, but the things you are willing to walk away from. The Rev. Dr. Martin Luther King said it this way, *"Faith is taking the first step when you can't find the staircase."*[41]

You need to know that when there is a call on your life, you will not be able to remain stationary. Any person who has authentically heard the voice of God had to move from where they were and find where God was showing them. That's why you are restless with the status quo. That's why you feel in your spirit there is more for you to do. That's why your dreams won't let you sleep. That's why even though the job is good, you feel in your spirit it is time to move on. That's why you can't tolerate the same foolishness of old, or deal with the same folk of yesterday. It's not that you are ungrateful for where you are or not thankful for what you have accomplished. It's not that you are becoming uppity or unappreciative, it is that **you are in the process of transition.**

How dare we want more? How dare we do more? How dare we desire more after all that we have already been given? So, we settle for being living monuments to the past, when the whole purpose of our past was to prepare us to move forward into the future.

Transitions are not always easy. In fact, most of the time they are painful. But transition is also necessary. It is a vital and inevitable part of our lives. The laws of the universe teach us this. A caterpillar can't become a butterfly unless it goes through a transition. An oyster cannot produce a pearl unless it goes through transition. Tadpoles don't become frogs unless they go through transition. The mimic octopus goes through transition in order to protect itself from its predators. David Banner doesn't become the superhero the Incredible Hulk, unless he goes through transition. Even Clark Kent must take off his glasses and suit to become Superman. Transitions are not always easy, but they are necessary.

Embracing Transition:
The Power of Showing Up

Intuitively, I think, people know that transition will cost them something. This is why they want to remain in the old season. There are three major mindsets that keep us from transitioning into something new.

Mindset #1: COMFORT: We often opt for comfort and convenience over the challenge of transition. Yet, Paul reminds us: *"12 Not that I have already obtained this or have already reached the goal,[a] but I will press on to lay hold of that for this Christ[b] has laid hold of me. 13 Brothers and sisters, I do not consider that I have laid hold[c] of it, but one thing I have laid hold of: forgetting what lies behind and straining forward to what lies ahead, 14 I press on toward the goal, toward the prize of the heavenly[d] call of God in Christ Jesus.42"*

Mindset #2: FEAR: People are afraid of the unknown. What makes a movie suspenseful is not knowing what will happen next. After you have already seen the movie, the scenes lose their ability to frighten you.

Say this with me: ***Quit looking backwards. Even when you can't figure out how to go forward, at least face forward.***

So often, we are wondering where God is and when God is going to show up. When the problem actually might be we are looking for God in the wrong direction. Maybe we need to consider the fact that God is not just working behind us or in front of us, God is working all around us.

You know the story. The Israelites started to panic because the Red Sea was in front of them and their past was chasing behind them. Yet, the Bible says that the angel of the Lord who was going before the Israelites moved and went behind them; and the pillar of cloud moved from in front of them and took its place.

In other words, the persuasive power of God shifted from the front to the back and created a barrier between the Israelites and their enemies. And the one thing I love about God is, God is everywhere. Yet fear tends to create a flawed perspective of reality. And when you have a flawed perspective of reality, it can make you blind to the persuasive presence of God.

Mindset #3: SENTIMENTALITY: Some people don't transition because they would rather live in yesterday's familiar, than walk forward into today's new revelation. They are content to live in yesterday's victory, rather than having to fight for a new victory today. Yet, **if you are ready for something new**, if you are ready to receive a new revelation from God, if you are ready to move past sentimentality, if you find yourself in transition, **accept that transition is inevitable.**

Transition in life is going to happen whether you like it or not, so you might as well make the best of it. The writer Ecclesiastes says it beautifully: *"For everything there is a season, and a time for every matter under heaven."*[43] This wisdom reminds us that life is full of cycles and changes, each with its own purpose and timing.

I call this process of navigating transition the "Power of Showing Up." This process is not about perfection, but about committed presence and action. It's about being there, fully engaged, even when the road ahead is uncertain.

Here is how you can put this process into action:

- **Identify Your Seeds:** Reflect on the small actions you can take today that align with your long-term vision. These seeds may seem insignificant, but they are the foundation upon which your dreams will grow.

- **Embrace Imperfect Action:** Don't wait for the perfect moment. Start now, learn, and adjust as you go. Risk is an inevitable part of the transition process. See this time as an opportunity to display your faith. See this time as God's way of surprising you with something better, something bigger.

- **Cultivate Resilience:** Prepare for challenges by focusing on progress, not perfection. Remember, it's not about being flawless; it's about moving forward with purpose.

- **Expect Resistance:** It's going to happen. Don't let this catch you off guard. People are going to be critical. Expect some anxiety and confusion to try to sneak in. This is all a necessary part of the process. Without these things, there would be no victory.

- **Dream and Do:** As you navigate life's transitions, it's crucial to balance visionary thinking with practical, daily actions. This isn't just about having big dreams; it's about taking tangible steps towards making them a reality. When shifts and transitions shake you to the core, see that as a sign of the greatness that's about to occur. It's in these moments that you discover your strength and God's provision. So, don't just dream, do. Don't just envision the future, take practical steps to get there. This balance between visionary thinking and practical doing is not just a strategy, it's a necessity. It's the bridge that connects your aspirations to your achievements. It's the catalyst that turns your dreams into a reality.

Abram, at the time of this text, is a successful merchant in Haran. He is settled. His family is secure. His future is comfortable. Yet, when God calls him, Abram finds himself in a season of transition. God tells him to leave all that he knows behind him and to go to the land that God will show him. And that's how God works sometimes. **God will call you to walk away from some things, even successful things, when they don't match your divine assignment.**

God said to Abram, *"Where I'm getting ready to take you, I'm not even going to tell you the name of the place. And the reason I'm not telling you the name of the place is because I need you to be committed to me, even when you don't have all the answers."* And here's the tension for us as believers, real faith is following God, even when your questions outweigh your certainty and your destination remains unclear.

I hear the rational person in you saying to God, how am I going to start over at this age? How am I going to leave this good job to start that business or go back to school? How am I going to follow my dreams with all the responsibilities I have? How am I going to walk away from this relationship? I know it's destroying me but it's all I have. It's all I know.

And God is simply replying to us, "Go!" Go to the land that I will show you. You might stumble but you won't fall down. Go to the land that I will show you. There are no time limits on my promises for you. Go to the land that I will show you. What seems impossible for some is not impossible for me. Go to the land that I will show you. I don't give you dreams based upon your size right now; I give you dreams based upon your destiny.

Sometimes, the only thing standing between us and the life God dreams for us is the courage to take that first step. And that's the issue for many of us. We aren't where we're meant to be, not because God didn't have a plan for us, but simply because we didn't take the step to go.

The Bible says: Now the lord said to Abram, *"Go from your country, your people, and your father's household to the land I will show you."* God doesn't just whisper "go." God calls us to move now, to risk, to trust, and to discover His presence in the unknown.

Faith is never safe. Faith is like a wild river, not a placid pond. Every act of faith means letting go of what you can see and grasping for what you can't. Every leap of faith is a letting go of comfort, of control, and of what is visible, for the invisible.

The writer of Ecclesiastes 10:8 reminds us: *"When you work in a quarry, stones might fall and crush you. When you chop wood, there is danger with each stroke of your ax! Such are the risks of life."*[44]

In other words, there is no path worth walking that doesn't demand courage. To follow God is to trade the safety of the shore for the adventure of the open sea. The real question isn't whether risk is required, but whether we will trust the One who calls us out upon the waters.

I'm reminded of the movie, Indiana Jones and the Last Crusade. This is the third movie in the Indiana Jones franchise and Harrison Ford returned to the title role with Sean Connery playing his father. The story goes that the intrepid explorer, Indiana Jones, sets out to rescue his father, a medievalist who vanished while searching for the Holy Grail. Following clues in the old man's notebook, Indy arrives in Venice, where he enlists the help of a beautiful academic, but they are not the only ones who are on the trail, and some sinister old enemies soon come out of the woodwork. In the movie, there is a scene where Indiana Jones comes to the edge of a cliff. He is challenged to step over the cliff even though he can't see a bridge in front of him. Even though the bridge is not visible, Indiana Jones takes one step, and the bridge appears under his feet. He takes another step, and another plank of the bridge appears beneath his feet. You get the point; with each step, a new plank appears beneath his feet. That's how faith works. Faith is stepping out and doing what God has asked you to do even when you can't see what will happen in the end.

The writer of Hebrews defines faith this way: *"faith is the substance of things hoped for; the evidence of things not seen."*[45] In other words, **faith is trusting God enough to obey what He has said, and hope is having the confidence that God will do everything that He has promised.** Faith pushes us beyond our comfort zones; hope pulls us toward God.

Many times, we'll come to the edge of faith in our own lives. We're not sure where things are headed. Maybe it is a decision to start a relationship with Jesus for the first time. Maybe you need to trust him with a business decision, or something related to a relationship. Will you trust in the Lord with all your heart? What if you're wrong? Is it really God telling you to take the step of faith?

If that's your story, let me introduce you to the 80/20 principle. Vilfredo Federico Damaso Pareto was born in Italy in 1848. He would go on to become an important philosopher and economist. Legend has it that one day he noticed that 20% of the pea plants in his garden generated 80% of the healthy pea pods. This observation caused him to think about uneven distribution. He thought about wealth and discovered that 80% of the land in Italy was owned by just 20% of the population. He investigated different industries and found that 80% of production typically came from just 20% of the companies. The generalization became: 80% of results will come from just 20% of the action. This "universal truth" about imbalance of inputs and outputs is what became known as the Pareto principle, or the 80/20 rule. While it doesn't always come to be an exact 80/20 ratio, the imbalance is often seen in various business cases: 20% of the sales reps generate 80% of the total sales; 20% of customers account for 80% of total profits. Yet, I'm not talking about a business principle. I'm talking about a faith principle.

I'm talking about you doing 80 percent of God's will that's clear in the Bible and letting God show you the 20 percent that's not clear. In other words, you do the 80 percent. Love your neighbor as you love yourself. Spend time in God's word. Talk to God in prayer. Spend time with God's people. Love your family. Love your kids. Protect the way you speak to people. Be kind in your relationships. Be patient and let God do the 20 percent. Let God be the dream giver and you be the dream doer. Let God take what the enemy meant for evil and use it for your good.[46] Let God do in your life exceedingly abundantly above all that you can ask or think.[47] Let God be your refuge and your strength, a very present help in times of trouble.[48] Let God be your dwelling place in all generations.[49] Let God be your strong tower; the righteous run into it and are safe.[50] Let God be your king, your rock and your sustainer. Let God be your light in the darkness. Let

God direct your steps. Let God be your joy in the time of sorrow. Let God be your today and your tomorrow. And let God be your light, your deliverer and your redeemer.

Everything in life is a risk. Love is a risk. Following your heart is a risk. Yielding to God's will is a risk. Growing beyond what you know is a risk. Starting over is a risk. **Dreaming again is a risk. But playing it safe is risky too!** God says to Abram "now." God says to Abram "go." God says to Abram "risk." And finally, God says to Abram "BELIEVE." Even when the path is unclear.

William Tyndale had a dream of translating the Bible into English. The church opposed his work, even putting a bounty on his head. Tyndale taught himself Hebrew in order to translate the Old Testament. Then, he worked feverishly from dawn to dusk, six days a week, for eleven years until the translation was completed because he had an unwavering belief in his dream.[51]

Louis L'Amour had a dream of being a writer. The publishing world did not share his dream. He received 350 rejections before he made his first sale. He persisted until finally one of his books was published, the first of over 200 western novels written which have sold over 200 million copies because he had an unwavering belief in his dreams.[52]

Charles Schultz had a dream of being an artist. But he had a bad start. As an awkward kid with a bad complexion who barely graduated from high school, Schultz submitted cartoons to the high school annual which were rejected. He was told by his teacher he could not draw children, but he persisted until he became one of the best-known cartoonists in the world because he had an unwavering belief in his dreams.[53]

What I love about Abram is that when God calls him, he doesn't hesitate. He doesn't delay. He doesn't ask God for credentials or for a money-back guarantee. He doesn't ask for a road map or Siri to guide him in the right direction. He doesn't ask God to consult with him regarding the people to take or the people to leave behind. He doesn't question his worthiness of the call, or fret about it being the right time, or the right moment in his life. He doesn't question God's motives, or God's abilities to do what He promised He would do. Verse 4 simply says *"Abram went as the Lord had told him."*[54]

Even When the Path is Unclear, Take a Step Forward Anyhow.

Even when the path is unclear, take a step forward anyhow. Even when you don't have all the answers, take a step forward anyhow. Even when doubt and confusion come into your life, take a step forward anyhow. I know this seems counterintuitive. Yet, one single step offers direction and creates momentum.

It was 1990, and Joanne Rowling, who we now know as J.K. Rowling, was riding a train from Manchester to London. The train was delayed, and as she gazed out the window, an idea fluttered into her mind: a boy with messy hair, round glasses and a lightning bolt-shaped scar who didn't know he was a wizard. She could see him so clearly; it was as if he was sitting in the seat beside her. But she had no pen, no paper, just her imagination and four long hours to let the story unfold in her mind.

When she finally stepped off that train, she carried with her the seed of a world that would one day enchant millions. But at that moment, her life was anything but magical. Over the next few years, Rowling's journey would be marked by hardship. She moved to Portugal, fell in love, married, had a daughter. But the marriage ended, and she returned to the UK as a single mother, carrying little more than a suitcase and the first three chapters of her story.

She settled in Edinburgh, struggling to make ends meet. Money was tight. She wrote in Cafes, her baby daughter asleep in the pram beside her, the clink of teacups and the hum of conversation her daily soundtrack. There were days when the weight of her circumstances felt unbearable, when the world seemed to whisper that her dream was foolish, impossible, and out of reach.

But Rowling kept writing. Not because she was certain of success, but because she loved the story and believed in the boy wizard she had met on the train. She sent her manuscript to publisher after publisher. Twelve times, she was told no. Twelve times, her dream was left waiting at the door. And then, finally, a small publisher named Bloomsbury said yes. The first print run was tiny, just 500 copies. But that was all it took. Harry Potter burst into the world, and so did Rowling's dream, no longer waiting, but alive and growing.

J.K. Rowling's story reminds us that **our dreams don't disappear when life gets difficult. They wait for us. They wait for us to believe in them, to nurture them, to take that first step,** even if it's just picking up a pen, or writing a single page, or daring to hope one more time.

Abram could have doubted God's call. Abram could have doubted God's vision for his life. And that's what doubt is. **Doubt is a side effect of having a desire to change and having a contrary thought that it just won't happen.** Yet, let me encourage you. It's time to let go of the thought that it won't happen. It's time to let go of the thought that you are not worthy. It's time to get really clear on what you want. It's time to believe and trust God and tell yourself with God's help and the Holy Spirit's guidance, nothing is impossible. Now watch the confusion fade. Now watch the doubt subside. Now watch the fear go away.

What I'm getting ready to say isn't for everybody. It's for the believers who know that for God, money is not an issue. It's for the believers who hear what the doctors say but know what the Lord can do. It's for the believers who know that "nothing is impossible for God." It's for the believers who know that God can promote you over folk more qualified than you. It's for the believers who know that God loves when His children dream big. It's for the believers who know that God never gives you a dream that matches your budget.

Are you ready for it? **Here it is: When there is an anointing on your life, it's not too late, it's never too late, to dream again.** Some of you might be disappointed by the simplicity of my statement but my message for you is simply this: It's not too late. It's never too late to give your life to Christ. It's never too late to walk in God's vision for your life. It's never too late for God to do a new thing in your life. It's never too late for God to work a miracle in your life. It's never too late to dream again! Because when you give yourself permission to dream again, big things happen!

It's Never Too Late! Trusting in God's Timing.

The Bible says that Abram was 75 years old when God called him. That tells me that you are never too old, the goal is never too great, and the obstacles are never too high when you are doing God's will. If God gave you a dream, God is big enough, mighty enough and great enough to make your dreams come true.

So, let me ask you: Are you ready to trust in God's timing? If so, don't let age, or doubt or fear hold you back. Life is full of stories of those who achieved greatness later in life. Just look at Barbara Hillary reaching the north pole at 75 and the south pole at 79. Just look at Fauja Singh running marathons at 100. Just look at Julia Child becoming a culinary icon at 50. Their stories remind us that **purpose doesn't come with an expiration date and destiny isn't confined to a set season. The pen is in your hands, and your story is yours to write.** So, start writing it today. And here's what you will discover: **"your now" is not just a promise. It's a reality waiting to unfold.**

The Bible says, God told Abram: *"I know it's hard to let go. I know walking away from old places and familiar faces is difficult to do. I saw how others settled in Haran, and I know you carry the burden of a Daddy who gave up too soon. But if you trust me, if you dare to believe in me, this is the smallest you will ever be."*

And beloved, that's what Jesus is saying to you: *"If you believe in me, I will be your protector, your sustainer, your provider, your problem solver, your healer, and your savior. The dream that God placed within you is not too bold, and the vision that God gave you is not too audacious. All you need to do is to take that first trembling step, no matter how small or uncertain it feels. Because on the other side of your faith, your dreams are waiting for you to show up. So, don't let them wait any longer. It's time for you to step out and meet them."*

CHAPTER 6
There's a Reason You're Not Alone

Genesis 12:4-6

⁴So Abram went, as the Lord had told him, and Lot went with him. Abram was seventy-five years old when he departed from Haran. ⁵Abram took his wife Sarai and his brother's son Lot and all the possessions that they had gathered and the persons whom they had acquired in Haran, and they set forth to go to the land of Canaan. When they had come to the land of Canaan, ⁶Abram passed through the land to the place at Shechem, to the oak[a] of Moreh. At that time the Canaanites were in the land.

One of the great things about having children is that if you are paying close enough attention, living with them usually presents you with a teachable moment. Years ago, when my son, Charles III, was seven years old, I remember him running up to me with excitement in his eyes after one of his basketball games that he played exceptionally well.

"Daddy, Daddy did you count how many points I scored? Did you see how I led the fast break? Did you see how I broke that kid's ankles when I dribbled up the lane, made a cross-over to my left and stopped and hit the fade away jumper? I don't know about you Daddy, but you better tell Coach Heard he better come get me. Your boy is about to blow up!"

I smiled to myself, and with pride only a father knows, I looked at my son and said these words: "You played a great game, son. You have a lot of potential. You scored over 20 points. There were times they couldn't guard you. And I'm not saying this because I'm your father, but I truly believe if you work hard and dedicate yourself to the game, BIG things can happen for you. Who knows, maybe one day you will be playing in the NBA.

But son, let me ask you a question. Do you remember the defense that your team played that led to your fast breaks and your open jump shots? Do you remember how hard your team played around you to put you in a position to win? I would be the first to say that I don't know much about basketball but one thing I do know: "Individuals win games, but teams win championships." And from my own experience of working in corporate America for over 20 years, from leading teams of people, from building and running million-dollar businesses, from launching a local church with no staff and no money, to pastoring a growing ministry, you may be good, but you are only as good as the team around you.

I must admit, when I said that last statement, I popped my own collar. In my mind, I know I had said something significant. I had made a strong argument. I had proven my case. I had given him logical and cogent illustrations that tied back to what he knew. But sometimes I forget who I'm dealing with. My son was seven. And sometimes talking to a seven-year-old is not about logic, it's about the unexpected. So, when I asked Charles if he understood what I was saying, he replied to me this way: *"Yes, Daddy. But I have a question."* A question for me, I thought. I got excited. My chest puffed out. He heard me. My point resonated with him. "What's your question, son?" And he looked me in the eyes and politely asked, *"Can I have my snack now?"*

While the story is funny, the moral is so true: **You may be good. You may be talented. You may have tremendous potential. You may even work hard. But you are only as good as the team around you.**

Let me say it this way: Even the Lone Ranger had Tonto. Batman had Robin. Tom had Jerry. Mickey Mouse had Minnie Mouse. Michael Jordan had Scottie Pippen. Ronald Reagan had Tip O'Neal. Kobe had Shaq. Even Superman had Louis Lane. No one is a Lone Ranger. Check the history books; search the internet. I am convinced you will not find one person who has done something of great significance alone.

That's why **when it comes to success, the people on your team often determine the height and breadth of your greatness.** And that's my critical question for you today: Who's on your team?

Do you have "Helpers" or do you have "Hinderers"? The helpers are the people who can propel you to the next level. Or do you have hinderers on your team? They are the people who try to block your flow. If they are miserable, they want you to be miserable too.

Who's on your team? Do you have "Enablers," or do you have "Encouragers"? The enablers are the Yes-Men who like you unfocused. They like you undisciplined. They like you immature because the more you depend on them, the more control they have over you. Or do you have encouragers on your team? They are the people who are bold enough to tell you the truth when you need it. They are the people who care about you enough to tell you sometimes that your stuff does stink. And they are the people who love you enough to push you to be your very best.

Who's on your team? Do you have "Leeches," or do you have "Lifters"? The leeches are the people who drain you of all you have to offer. They drain your resources. They drain your joy. They drain your spirit. They drain your enthusiasm, and once you don't have any more to give them, they drop you in search of the next sucker. Or do you have lifters on your team? The lifters are the people who don't want anything from you but instead want something for you. The lifters are the ones who want you to succeed. The lifters are the ones who want you to dream big. They want you to accomplish your goals. They want you to walk in God's glory for your life. They are not intimidated by you or jealous of you, because for them, it's not about who gets the shine. It's about God getting the glory.

Who's on your team? Do you have "Talkers," or do you have "Doers"? The talkers are the people who talk loudly but say nothing. They always have something to say. They are always ready to tell you what to do. But when it's time to work, when it's time to sacrifice, when it's time to roll up your sleeves and make it happen, they are the dead weight you carry. They are the people who can identify all the problems but never stick around long enough to help you create solutions. Or do you have doers on your team? They are the people that work with you and pray with you. They are the people that walk with you and sacrifice with you. They are the people who cry and laugh with you. They are the people who share and live in community with you. For, like you, they know the vision is bigger than you; it's bigger than them.

Who's on your team? That's the question that arrested my critical thinking. The Bible says: "*So, Abram went, as the Lord had told him; and Lot went with him. Abram was seventy-five years old when he departed from Haran. Abram took his wife Sarai and his brother's son Lot, and all the possessions that they had gathered, and the persons whom they had acquired in Haran; and they set forth to go to the land of Canaan."*[55] *And clause A of verse 6 says, "When they had come to the land of Canaan..."*

In other words, not only did Abram leave Haran for the land that God would show him. He made it to the Promised Land.

Growing up, one of my favorite television shows was "The Jeffersons" one of America's long running sitcoms. The show was a spin-off from "All in The Family" on which the Jeffersons were the neighbors or Archie and Edith Bunker. The show focused on George and Louise Jefferson, a prosperous black couple who were able to move from Queens to Manhattan owing to the success of George's dry-cleaning chain. For 11 years, I couldn't wait for the show to come on CBS with its iconic opening theme, "Movin' On Up" co-composed and performed by Ja'net DuBois. I pause here for a moment to congratulate those of you who, like George and Louise Jefferson, have made it to the east side. You have made it to the deluxe apartment in the sky. You have finally got a piece of the pie. It took a whole lotta trying just to get up that hill. But now you are in the big leagues getting your turn at bat and I want you to know, ain't nothing wrong with that. I celebrate you. I support you. I thank God for you. Because your success is a testimony to me; if God can do it for you, God can do it for me.

The Bible says Abram went as the Lord had told him. And despite his age and his history, where he came from and where he started, Abram made it to the Promised Land. But notice what the author says: he didn't make it there alone. He had a team around him. He had his wife on his team. He had his nephew on his team. He even had the people he had acquired in Haran on his team. But besides being a good story, what is God trying to tell us?

First, the Bible says Abram takes with him the people that he acquired in Haran. On a cursory reading, this fact is interesting but not particularly newsworthy. But the more I read the text, the more I kept asking myself, "Why would Abram take anyone from Haran with him?" I can see him taking the money. I can see him taking the stuff he accumulated. But why would he take people? Didn't God tell him to leave his country, his father's house and his kindred and go to the land God would show him?

I didn't see it at first. But when I saw the answer, I must admit it almost blew my mind. You see, Abram knew something that some of us need to learn about life: **no one achieves anything great, alone. Because inevitably, we all get stuck.** Some of you know what I'm talking about. You are stuck in Haran. You are stuck in routine, stuck in fear, stuck in mediocrity, stuck in a dead-end job, stuck in disappointments, stuck in tradition, stuck in legalism, stuck in old mindsets, stuck in old habits, stuck in regret, stuck in false expectations. You are frustrated. You are not where you want to be, nor are you where you could be. But you have heard God's voice telling you to go. You have felt God's hand upon your life. You have seen the vision that God has for your life. But you are stuck.

That's the advantage you have over non-believers. That's one of the reasons that you're not alone. God is getting ready to send someone into your life that will help you reach the destiny God has for you. No one person ever has all of the answers. But when you are in community, you don't have to have all of the answers, for two heads are better than one. Former Supreme Court Justice, Sandra Day O'Connor said it this way, *"We don't accomplish anything in this world alone...and whatever happens is the result of the whole tapestry of one's life and all the weavings of individual threads from one to another that creates something."*

There are no true solo acts. If someone tells you they got where they are all by themselves, they're lying. Don't believe them, and don't buy what they're selling. None of us pull ourselves up by our bootstraps. Someone had to teach you to tie your own shoes. None of us get where we are going alone. There are certainly times of solitude and loneliness on the entrepreneurial, creative, artistic, professional, and personal pathways, but we are not really all by ourselves. There is always a crowd of people cheering you on, opening doors for you, and working behind the scenes to support your purpose. The quicker that you recognize this, the sooner you can embrace the power that comes in the potential of community.

We all get stuck sometimes. Days you want to give out. Days you want to give up. Days you want to cry. Days that nothing you do seems right. But isn't that why some of us have a personal trainer? No matter how much you know about fitness and no matter how fit you are, we all need someone to push us beyond our comfort zones.

I want to be your spiritual personal trainer today. And right where you are, reading this book, right in the condition you are in, right in the situation you are trying to solve, I want you to know, "I'm here for you." I'm here to support you. I'm here to challenge you. I'm here to encourage you to be all that God wants you to be. I hope you can receive this word in the spirit that I'm saying it, "I'm here for you." That's how lives are changed. That's how transformation occurs. That's how vision comes to life. That's how we accomplish our goals. That's how we change the world. God's people come together and tell the broken and the fallen and the person who needs encouragement and support to fulfil their God-sized opportunity, "I'm here for you."

The Bible says Abram takes with him the people of Haran and his brother's son Lot. To appreciate the point, you must understand the context. Chapters 11 and 12 tell us that Lot was raised by his uncle Abram, one of the greatest role models of godly character the Bible has to offer. But once Lot parted ways with Abram in chapter 13, he lost focus and direction. Remember that it was Lot who demanded his share of the blessing and headed to the land of Sodom and Gomorrah. And instead of imitating the faithfulness to God he witnessed in his uncle Abram, Lot spent the rest of his life following the path of least resistance. When Lot got in trouble, it was Abram in chapter 14 who went to war against the enemies of Sodom and Gomorrah and won his release through battle. And in chapter 19, when the angels of the Lord appeared to Lot and warned him that his sins would lead to his ruin, it was Lot who refused to leave. And as a result, Lot got himself in some mess that he couldn't redeem himself from.

My point of sharing Lot's story is simply this. **No matter how much you love someone, you can't want more for them than they want for themselves.** We all have people on our team that we love to death. Maybe Mama is on our team. Maybe Daddy is on our team. Maybe sister, brother, cousin, daughter, son or friend is on our team, and if that is the case, that's great. Because no one achieves greatness on their own. But never forget, you can't want more for Johnnie than Johnnie wants for himself. If Johnnie wants to play video games and you want to make something of your life, then fine. Leave Johnnie at home.

You can't want more for your child than they want for themselves. If your child wants to be average and ordinary, I know it breaks your heart, but that's their choice. It's their life. Don't you take responsibility for grown folk's decisions. If all your girl wants to do is wear $5 dresses and have any warm body in her bed when she can have a real man who loves her, honors her, respects her and takes care of her. All I have to say is that she will always be your girl, but some foolishness you don't have to put up with.

I know it sounds cold but it's the truth. There are some folks who will get you here, but they can't get you there. You love them and you want the best for them, but once you reach this goal, or this plateau, they may not be the folk with you on the next adventure that God gives you. The mark of any great leader or someone going somewhere or someone growing for God's glory, is to be able to critically and objectively evaluate who is on your team. I feel this in my spirit, something BIG is happening in your life, but the old proverb is true: **you are only as strong as your weakest link.**

I know that might sound like a cliché. Yet, when looking at all the major components within your life, such as health and wellness, career, relationships, community, faith and finances, they are all individual, important links in the overall chain of your life that pulls you toward a higher level. As you take the time to improve one area, if you are not neglecting or being oblivious to the others, all others in your life will improve, strengthening the overall tension available within the chain. In other words, the strength in a chain is provided when tension is placed on it. This tension is represented in your life with things like obstacles and challenges that are pushing you to become your best and reach a higher level. They are work challenges that demand your best. They are family issues that make you step up to the task of being a great parent, or spouse. They are community activities that require your time and commitment in giving back. What's your weakest link? Is it making you better, or is it making you weaker?

The Bible says Abram takes with him the people from Haran, the stuff he acquired, his nephew Lot and his wife Sarai. And again, that makes sense. Sarai was his wife. She followed him from Ur to Haran. Why wouldn't she be on his expedition team to the Promised Land? But the writer throws a twist in the story. In Genesis 12:2, God promises to make a great nation through Abram and Sarai.

But where are my critical readers? Something does not compute. Because in Genesis 11:30, the Bible says: *"Sarai was barren; she had no child."*

Now, I am not a doctor, nor do I profess to be one on TV, but it doesn't take a medical degree to know that something great can't come from a barren place. And to make matters worse, history records that for a married woman in Biblical times, being barren is about the worst thing that could ever happen in your life! Barren women were ostracized. Barren women were overlooked. Barren women were mocked by everyone as being unfruitful!

This reminds me of a conversation I had with a friend of mine. I told him that I couldn't understand how a friend of ours could let himself go. In over a year, he gained so much weight he became unrecognizable. Unfortunately, we teased him. We shamed him. We harassed him to lose weight. But the more we did it, the more weight he seemed to gain. Then one day his wife said something to me that has stuck with me ever since. She said, *"Don't think you are better than Tim. His issues are obvious. Your issues are hidden."*

Can I help you? We all have points of barrenness. We all have some places that will not grow. We all have some issues we can't shake. We all have some blind spots that we cannot see. We all have some sins we have committed. But that's the point that God wants to make through Sarai. Even with your barrenness, I've got you. Even when people overlook you, I see you. Even when people laugh at you and don't value you, I can still use you. That's why you are not alone, because even in the barren seasons of your life, you need to know that God has you. God sees you. God can still use you.

Despite her age and despite her barrenness, Sarai still conceived and bore a son named Isaac. In

Matthew Chapter 1, the Gospel writer says: *"Abram was the father of Isaac. And Isaac was the father of Jacob. And Jacob was the father of Judah. And Judah was the grandfather of Jesse. And Jesse was the father of King David. And King David was the great, great grandfather of Joseph. And Joseph was the father of Jesus."*[56]

That's the reason you are not alone. Not only because of the people on your team. It's because of the savior you have in your life.

We have a Savior in Jesus who sticks to us closer than a brother. We have a Savior in Jesus who can speak life into our dead situations. We have a Savior in Jesus who can calm the storms that rage in our lives. We have a Savior in Jesus who bore our sin. We have a Savior in Jesus who died on an old, rugged cross that we might have peace, that we might have hope, that we might know love, that we might experience joy. And we have a Savior in Jesus who not only cancels our sins but gives us salvation through his resurrection power.

That's how we can proclaim as believers: Even in my weakness, Jesus' grace is still sufficient. Even through the valley, Jesus is the lamp upon my feet. Even in my dry places, Jesus is my living water. Even in my barren places, Jesus is a way-maker. Even when the sun refuses to shine in this sinful life of mine, Jesus is my redeemer. Even when I'm down to my very last dime, Jesus is my sustainer. Even when I have fallen and can't get up, Jesus is my lifter. Even in my distress, Jesus is my balm in Gilead.[57] Even in my confusion, Jesus is my compass. Even when I find myself in my feelings, Jesus is faithful. That's why I give Him glory! That's why I give Him praise! That's why we worship Him! We are never alone. We have a Savior named Jesus in our lives.

Mary Jane "Jennie" Bain Wilson was born on a farm in Cleveland, Indiana in 1856, the younger daughter of Robert Wilson and Mary Frances Russel Wilson. Her father died in her infancy. When she was about four years old, an attack of spinal trouble resulted in her being rendered an invalid, confined to a wheelchair and bed. Not being able to attend school, she studied at home, read much, and received some musical instruction. Yet, despite all that she endured, she knew by faith she was never alone. That's how she could write this great hymn of the church, "Hold to God's Unchanging Hands."[58]

1. *Time is filled with swift transition,*
   Naught of earth unmoved can stand,
   Build your hopes on things eternal,
   Hold to God's unchanging hand.
   Refrain:
   Hold to God's unchanging hand,
   Hold to God's unchanging hand;
   Build your hopes on things eternal,

Hold to God's unchanging hand.

2. *Trust in Him who will not leave you,*
   Whatsoever years may bring,
   If by earthly friends forsaken,
   Still more closely to Him cling.

3. *Covet not this world's vain riches,*
   That so rapidly decay,
   Seek to gain the heav'nly treasures,
   They will never pass away.

4. *When your journey is completed,*
   If to God you have been true,
   Fair and bright the home in glory,
   Your enraptured soul will view.

There's a reason you are not alone. When the glory of the Lord falls upon you, when the blessings of the King become available to you, when you boldly walk in the vision that God has for your life, when your life is marked by progress and not just potential, you will be able to say without a shadow of doubt, nobody but Jesus did it. Nobody but Jesus did it!

CHAPTER 7
Faith Beyond the Horizon

Genesis 13:1-18
Abram and Lot Separate

13 So Abram went up from Egypt, he and his wife and all that he had and Lot with him, into the Negeb.2 Now Abram was very rich with livestock, in silver, and in gold.3 He journeyed on by stages from Negeb as far as Bethel, to the place where his tent had been at the beginning, between Bethel and Ai, 4to the place where he had made an altar at the first, and there Abram called on the name of the Lord. 5Now Lot, who went with Abram, also had flocks and herds and tents, 6and the land could not support both of them living together because their possessions were so great that they could not live together. 7Thus strife arose between the herders of Abram's livestock and the herders of Lot's livestock. At that time the Canaanites and the Perizzites lived in the land.

8Then Abram said to Lot, "Let there be no strife between you and me and between your herders and my herders, for we are kindred. 9Is not the whole land

128

before you? Separate yourself from me. If you take the left hand, then I will go to the right, or if you take the right hand, then I will go to the left." ¹⁰Lot looked about him and saw that the plain of the Jordan was well watered everywhere like the garden of the Lord; like the land of Egypt, in the direction of Zoar; this was before the Lord destroyed Sodom and Gomorrah. ¹¹So Lot chose for himself all the plain of Jordan, and Lot journeyed eastward, and they separated from each other. ¹²Abram settled in the land of Canaan, while Lot settled among the cities of the plain and moved his tent as far as Sodom. ¹³Now the people of Sodom were wicked, great sinners against the Lord.

¹⁴The Lord said to Abram, after Lot separated from him, "Raise your eyes now, and look from the place where you are, northward and southwards and eastward and westward, ¹⁵for all the land that you see I will give to you and to your offspring forever. ¹⁶I will make your offspring like the dust of the earth, so that if one can count the dust of the earth, your offspring also can be counted. ¹⁷Rise up, walk through the length and the breadth of the land, for I will give it to you." ¹⁸So Abram moved his tent and came and settled by the oaks[a] of Mamre, which are at Hebron, and there he built an altar to the Lord.

Let's be honest. Sometimes the hardest thing in life is knowing when to leave. Many of us have paid a high price for staying in places, relationships, or situations that no longer serve us. We've sacrificed our peace, our joy, and even our sanity because we thought everything had to last forever. But what if God's greatest blessings are waiting for us on the other side of letting go?

Abram's story doesn't begin with a thunderclap or a burning bush. It starts with a whisper, a promise so audacious it almost sounds like a dare. Leave everything, the voice says. Go to a place you've never seen and trust that something better is waiting. Most people would have rolled over and gone back to sleep. But not Abram. He packs up his life, leaves the familiar behind, and sets out on a 1,500-mile trek from Ur to Canaan, chasing a future only he can see.

He's not a superhero. He's a man with doubts, fears, and a stubborn hope that maybe, just maybe, the promise is real. Every time he sets up camp, or builds an altar, it's not just a religious ritual. It's a marker of survival, a signpost that says, "I made it this far." But the road isn't straight, and the promise doesn't come with a map.

Then comes Egypt. Egypt is the system, slick seductive, and utterly indifferent to Abram's private dreams. Famine hits, and suddenly the man of faith is improvising. He tells Sarai to say she is his sister. It's a small lie, but in Egypt, small lies have a way of growing teeth.59 The man who left everything for a whisper of destiny now finds himself gaming the system, just to survive.

If you read to the end of Genesis 12, you'll see the chaos that follows. Egypt is a place of confusion, where faith is tested, and mistakes are made. Abram is faithful, but he's not perfect. He stumbles, just as we all do. Egypt becomes a metaphor for those moments when we wander from God's will, when fear drives our decisions, and when we try to control outcomes instead of trusting God.

Let me be clear: **we all have our "Egypt."** Maybe you're in one right now. Maybe you've made choices out of fear, and now you're living with the consequences. But here's the hope. God doesn't abandon Abram in Egypt, and He won't abandon you. Even amid bad decisions, God's grace is at work, calling us back to His promises.

Everyone has an Egypt. Maybe yours is a job, a relationship, a secret you're sure you can manage. Maybe you're there now, improvising, hoping no one notices the cracks. But the story of Abram, told not as a sermon, but as a human drama, is that **you can always come back to God.**

The opening portion of Genesis chapter 13 reveals a profound truth about spiritual restoration. Abram knows he's messed up! So, he decides to retrace his steps to get back into a committed relationship with God and goes back to the place between Bethel and Ai. Bethel is the place where he had settled and built an altar before. Yet, returning to Bethel is not by happenstance. The first altar built in Shechem was God seeking Abram. But the altar he built between Bethel and Ai is Abram seeking God!

Do you see it now? Abram is trying to get things right! I can hear him saying to himself, "You know what? I need to get myself right. I need to go back to the place where I met God. I need to go back to the place where I had a unique and real tight relationship with God. I need to go back to that altar that I built."

And I want to suggest that's why YOU ought to build altars where you go because you never know when you're going to have to go back and remind yourself, GOD IS STILL FAITHFUL! God is still a keeper!

But as we keep reading Genesis 13, we realize that just when you think things are going well, just when you assume you've made it, just when you've got comfortable, problems arise for the duration of chapter 13. The text tells us the issue that arises, not with an enemy, but with his nephew. But the text tells us there comes a point in the relationship between Abram and Lot that they can no longer coexist with one another. And they make the mature decision that one needs to go their way and another needs to go the other way. And by the time this chapter ends, the Bible tells us that Lot and Abram, have separated.

But watch what takes place. Abram gives you and I what I think is a wonderful template about what it means to be spiritually mature. Because I would suggest to you that too many of us assume that you are only spiritually mature when you stay. But what if I told you that it takes spiritual maturity to walk away? I know you've been told that you just got to stick some stuff through. And that's good advice in certain seasons and situations of life because too often people hit the "abort button" when they need to hit the "stay button." But Abram teaches us that in certain moments in life, you must decide what you will accept, and what you will not accept. And the story goes that Abram comes to the moment and realizes that if he is to get all that God has for him, he must leave Lot behind.

I don't know who or what your Lot is. I'm not sure who or what you're connected to. I'm not sure what you're wrestling with. I'm not sure if Lot is a person, an opportunity or maybe something you don't think you can live without. But Abram teaches us that if you know that Lot ain't the Lord, you will be alright. Somebody can testify, as long as I got the Lord, I can live my life. As long as I got the Lord, I got everything I need. And that's what we see takes place here because Abram's decision teaches us that in critical seasons of life, we must make the mature decision; that for the sake of God's vision for our lives, we must be willing to separate from some things and some Lots so we can hear God clearly, so we can live faithfully, and so we can worship God freely. I think somebody needs to hear that again. **It's only when you leave your Lots behind, can you see God clearly, can you live faithfully, and you can worship God freely.**

What would you do if I told you that God sent me on an assignment to let you know that if you don't know how to manage your life, if you don't know how to handle your life, if you don't know how to separate from your Lots, you're going to be stuck where you are? And here's the crazy thing about it, you can be in the Promised Land and still be miserable.

As we examine the story of Abram and Lot, several powerful lessons emerge.

Lesson 1: Success can create tension, but it also reveals character.

As the sun blazed over the rugged hills, the land between Bethel and Ai shimmered with promise, and tension; when Abram and Lot settled in Bethel and Ai, both experienced prosperity. Abram had been blessed for years, and now Lot was also thriving; he had flocks, herds, and wealth of his own. However, this shared success led to tension between them. The land could not support both of their growing possessions, and soon, conflict arose between their herders.

This moment reveals a crucial truth: **prosperity often brings new challenges.** When everyone is struggling, unity comes more easily. But when resources multiply, differences and ambitions can surface. The relationship between Abram and Lot changed. Before, Lot had depended on Abram; he followed him out of Ur, through Egypt, and into

Canaan. Now, Lot was independently successful, and the dynamic shifted from dependence to rivalry.

Picture the sun rising over the hills between Bethel and Ai, painting the land gold, a land that once felt endless, now is suddenly crowded. Two men stand at the heart of the tension: Abram, the seasoned patriarch whose faith has carried him across deserts and kingdoms, and Lot, his nephew, no longer a mere follower but a man of wealth and ambition in his own right.

For years, Lot had walked in Abram's shadow, following him from Ur, through famine and fortune, always the apprentice to a master. But now, both men have prospered. Their herds multiply, their servants fill the valleys, and the land, once more than enough, begins to feel tight, like a room with too many voices and not enough air. The text tells us: "the land could not support them while they stayed together, for their possessions were so great that they were not able to stay together."

But beneath the surface, something more subtle and dangerous is at work. The relationship between Abram and Lot has shifted. Before, Lot depended on Abram. He followed him out of Ur, through Egypt, into Canaan. Now, Lot is independently successful. The dynamic is no longer mentor and protégé but equals; two men, each with their own ambitions, standing on their own feet. As long as the relationship was one-sided, there was peace. But now, with both men thriving, unspoken tensions rise.

The Spark of Conflict

It's not just Abram and Lot who feel the strain. Their herdsmen, the people loyal to each, begin to quarrel. The conflict isn't only about sheep and land; it's about identity, pride, and the challenge of coexistence when success is shared. Often, the friction doesn't start with the leaders, but with those around them – their people, their families, their communities. Sometimes, the people closest to us can't stand the changes that success brings, and their unrest spills over into our relationships. And **sometimes the greatest battles are fought not with swords, but with humility and open hands.**

Hidden Battles and Unseen Enemies

The text hints at another layer of drama: while Abram and Lot are internally feuding, external threats loom. The Canaanites and Perizzites still live in the land, waiting for a moment of weakness. The real danger isn't just the quarrel between uncle and nephew, but what happens when internal division leaves them vulnerable to outside forces. When we're not honest about the tension within, we risk weakening our defenses against the struggles around us.

Abram, with the wisdom of years and the humility of faith, steps into the breach. He refuses to let rivalry destroy family. "Let there be no strife between you and me...for we are brothers," he says. He gives Lot the first choice – a gesture that stuns, a sacrifice that echoes through generations. Lot, seeing the lush plans of the Jordan, chooses for himself, leaving Abram with the hills and the promise of God.

As Lot departs, the silence between the uncle and nephew is heavy. The land is divided, but so are their destinies. Lot's choice will lead him towards Sodom and its dangers. Abram's choice toward the unknown, but also toward his blessing.

Lesson 2: Sometimes you must be the one to take the first step.

The sun is beating down on the land, and the dust of many herds fills the air. Tension hangs thick and heavy, not just between Abram and Lot, but among everyone traveling with them. Every day, the arguments between their herdsmen grow louder, the glances sharper, the silence at mealtimes more uncomfortable. It's the kind of conflict that everyone hopes will just fade away if ignored long enough, but it doesn't. It festers, growing in the shadows.

Verse 8 tells us something interesting. Notice it starts with the words *"Let there be no strife between you and me."* If you were in the text, you would see the tension was going on for a while, to the point where everyone was just going along and letting it simmer. Maybe you've been there too, hoping that if you just wait, things will work themselves out. You don't want to rock the boat. You keep going along, thinking, "One day it's going to get better. One day it's going to work out." But you know, and I know, that things often don't work out by themselves. No matter how much you wish they would, no matter how much you hope people would change, sometimes, if you're not careful, you'll allow stuff to fester and continue.

But imagine Abram's internal struggle. He could have been resentful. After all, Lot owed so much to Abram: his wealth, his safety, even his presence in the land. Abram was the one called by God, the one who received the promise, the one who led them out of Ur. Lot was just going along for the ride, and now his herdsmen were causing trouble. Abram could've said, "After all I've done for you, this is how you repay me?" He could have insisted on his rights, demanded the best land, or sent Lot away in anger.

Instead, Abram chooses a different path. A path of humility, faith, and love. He lets go of resentment and steps forward to make peace, showing remarkable spiritual growth. He trusts God to provide, no matter the outcome. This is maturity: putting relationships above his rights, peace above pride.

Then Abram said to Lot, *"Let there be no strife between you and me, and between your herders and my herders; for we are kindred. Is not the whole land before you? Separate yourself from me. If you take the left hand, I will go to the right hand; or if you take the right hand, then I will go to the left hand."*[60]

Sometimes, just wishing things would get better isn't enough. Praying is important, but everything isn't just going to work out because you prayed about it. You also must act. Often, the responsibility to resolve conflict falls on the bigger person. After you take it to the Lord, you need to get up, go talk to the person, and work toward a resolution.

Here's my prayer: *"Lord, teach me how to say it the right way." When I was a kid, I was taught that "sticks and stones may break my bones, but words will never hurt me" – but that's not true. Words can hurt, and how you say something matters.*

What I appreciate about Abram is how he handles the situation. He finally gets to the point where he says, "You know what? I didn't start the issue but let me be the mature one. Let me try to bring a resolution to the situation. It isn't even my issue, but I'm going to go ahead and try." Sometimes, for the greater peace, you need to make the decision to take the first step. Bigger people understand that even if it isn't your fault, sometimes you must be the one to act.

Abram doesn't go accusing Lot. He doesn't go to talk about the issue to others. He goes directly to Lot, seeking understanding. He doesn't let the situation keep building. He doesn't allow the tension to keep growing. He knows it's not good for the community, not good for the family, not good for the people of God.

Maybe some of us need to do what Abram did, go to ourselves and ask, "Am I willing to be the bigger person? Am I willing to take the first step?" Because the truth is, sometimes we let things go on too long. We let resentment simmer, hoping time will fix what only honesty can heal. We walk on eggshells, we avoid the issue, we post vague messages on social media, but nothing changes. Some of us even like the tension, like the drama, but deep down, it's not what God wants for us.

So, let's step into Abram's sandals for a moment. Feel the tension, the uncertainty, the risk of being misunderstood. Hear the anxious murmurs of the herdsmen, see the worried faces of the families. And then, feel the relief and hope when Abram finally speaks up, not to win, but to reconcile.

Abram's willingness to address the problem directly, speak the truth in love, and offer a generous solution, diffuses the tension and preserves the unity of their family. And his actions remind us that peace is possible when someone is brave enough to act with grace and honesty.

Call to Action:

Who in your life do you need to approach today? Is there a conversation you've been avoiding, hoping it will resolve itself?

Like Abram, choose to be the bigger person. Value relationships over being right. And remember: **Sometimes the greatest act of faith isn't moving mountains – it's reaching across the divide and saying, "Let's find a way forward. Together."**

Lesson 3: Sometimes you must lose to win!

Abram stood on the ridge, the sun setting behind him, casting long shadows over the land stretched out below. Lot, his nephew, someone he loved deeply, stood beside him, eyes scanning the fertile valleys and rugged hills. The tension was thick, not with anger, but with the weight of a decision that would shape both of their destinies.

Abram broke the silence, his voice gentle but resolute: "Lot, you are family. I care for you like my own son. We've come far together, but now, our herds and people are too many for one place. There's no need for strife. I want peace between us, no bitterness. So, I'll let you choose first. If you go left, I'll go right. If you go right, I'll go left. I want you to have what you feel is best. I won't hold any hard feelings."

Abram doesn't rush him. He doesn't tell Lot what he should do. He simply lets Lot take his time, choose what he wants, because peace is greater than land and love is greater than pride. Lot looks around, sees the lush green Jordan valley, and he chooses what seems best, the land that looks good, that's big enough for his herds and people. Abram doesn't argue. He doesn't say, "I'm the oldest, that should be my land."

That's not how Abram does it. He says, "If you want the best, take the best." Because Abram understands that **sometimes you got to lose to win.**

I know. I know. This is a hard lesson to digest. I get it because I'm a winner too. I'm competitive too. Yet, I need you to lean in spiritually because sometimes you got to lose, to win. And I know it might not feel good at the time but sometimes you got to look like you have been taken advantage of, to progress forward.

Be careful, beloved. Don't let the wrong people get in your ear telling you "What they wouldn't do or wouldn't let happen." Sometimes, peace will get you farther than conflict and sometimes letting go will bless you more than trying to hold on.

Making It Personal

You may feel the tension in your life. Maybe you're in a situation where you're tempted to fight for what you think you deserve. Maybe you're worried someone will get the upper hand if you don't stand your ground. But Abram's story challenges you: Are you willing to trust that letting go can lead to something better?

Don't let pride or fear make your decisions for you. Sometimes, the most powerful thing you can do is step back, release your grip, and trust that what's meant for you will find you, even if it doesn't look like a victory at first.

A Modern Parallel

It's April and one of the things I love about this time of year, despite the flowers blooming and the days getting longer and warmer, is the NFL Draft. I love sports. And nothing makes me more excited than the drama of the teams deciding who they are going to pick to help their teams become more successful. One of the things I learned from the draft is that if you are a General Manager (GM) of a team, you don't always have the luxury of drafting a high pick. However, a savvy GM knows that there are still some moves they can make.

Sometimes, to get a better draft pick, they must give up some things. Sometimes it's trading away star players or future picks for the hope of a better tomorrow; sometimes the sacrifice of letting go is the only way to secure a brighter future. The same is true in life: **sometimes, the only way to step into your promise is to let go of what you're holding onto now.**

The Spiritual Principle:
You Can't Receive Until You Release

That's how it works with God. **God's blessings often wait on the other side of surrender.** Sometimes, you must walk away from what's comfortable, from what you've always known, to step into the next level God has for you. That's not easy. It takes guts. But one thing I've learned about walking with God: **for every exit, there is an entrance. And for every end, there is an opportunity for a new beginning.**

The story goes that Abram settles in the land of Canaan while Lot settled among the cities of the Plain. Yet, something interesting happens in verse 14: *"The Lord said to Abram, after Lot had separated from him, "Raise your eyes now, and look from the place where you are, northward and southward and eastward and westward, for all the land that you see I will give you and your offspring forever."*[61]

Did you catch it? As long as Lot was with Abram, God was silent. But as soon as Abram let go, God spoke. Sometimes you must let go of people, situations, or even old dreams, so you can hear what God has been waiting to say.

The Courage to Step Back

I end this chapter with this story. Lena stood at the edge of the small town she had always known, her suitcase heavy not just with clothes but with memories. The streets lined with familiar faces, the corner café where she spent countless afternoons, the sound of Sunday morning bells, they all tugged at her heart, urging her to stay. But deep within, she knew it was time to go.

She had spent years trying to convince herself that comfort meant happiness, that familiarity was enough. Yet, a part of her longed for something more, something she couldn't find in the quiet streets of her childhood home. There was a dream waiting beyond the horizon, calling her to step into the unknown.

As the bus rambled down the road, Lena watched her town fade into the distance. The ache of leaving was real, but so was the excitement. Letting go was never easy, but she understood now, new beginnings required leaving something behind. And in the emptiness where the past once held her, a future was waiting to be written.

So, she made the decision. She packed her bags, said her goodbyes, and stepped into the unknown. The journey was not easy. There were moments of doubt, times when loneliness crept into her heart. But with every step, she saw glimpses of God's faithfulness. New friendships blossomed, her work became meaningful, and her faith deepened.

As Lena stood in her new home, sunlight spilling through unfamiliar windows, she felt the ache of all she had left behind, a hollow space where memories once lived. Yet, in that emptiness, something extraordinary was taking root. She breathed deeply; the air tinged with hope and the faintest scent of possibility.

In the quiet, she could almost hear the echo of her own laughter, not from the past, but from a future she was beginning to believe in. Every fear she had faced, every step into the unknown, had brought her here; to a place where faith was not just a word, but a living, breathing force.

Lena realized then that courage wasn't always loud or bold; sometimes, it was the quiet decision to let go, to trust that what lay ahead could be even greater than what was left behind. And as she smiled, she knew: the story wasn't ending. It was just beginning, written in the ink of hope and the courage to step back, so she could leap forward into the life waiting for her to claim it.

I believe God wants to do the same things in your life. Abram's greatness wasn't grabbing the best for himself, but in his willingness to let go and trust that God's promise was bigger than any plot of land. That's the kind of faith that changes everything. That's the kind of courage that lets you dream again and step forward into the life waiting for you to claim it.

Key Takeaways:
This story isn't just about ancient herdsmen. It's a mirror for our own lives:

- **Sometimes the real conflict isn't with the other person, but with the people around us and within ourselves.**

- **Internal struggles can make us vulnerable to external threats.** If we're not honest about what's happening inside, we risk being overwhelmed by what's outside.

- **True greatness is measured not by what we possess, but by what we're willing to give up for peace.**

- **Faith beyond the horizon is the kind that lets you dream again,** that gives you the courage to step back – so you can leap forward into the life God is waiting to give you.

What happens when the land can't support you? When you're growing, maturing,

succeeding, how do you handle the tension that success brings?

Are there relationships in your life where success has brought tension? Are there unspoken struggles within your circle: family, friends, colleagues, that threaten your dreams? Like Abram, can you choose humility and peace, even if it means letting go of something you value?

Letting go, isn't losing. It's making room for something greater, something more.

Like, Abram, dare to trust, dare to release, and watch as God does more than you could ever imagine.

CHAPTER 8

When You Don't See It Happening

Genesis 15:1-6
God's Covenant with Abram

15 After these things the word of the Lord came to Abram in a vision, "Do not be afraid, Abram, I am your shield; your reward shall be very great." 2 But Abram said, "O Lord God, what will you give me, for I continue childless, and the heir of my house is Eliezer of Damascus?"[a] 3 And Abram said, "You have given me no offspring, so a slave born in my house is to be my heir." 4 But the word of the Lord came to him, "This man shall not be your heir; no one but your very own issue shall be your heir." 5 He brought him outside and said, "Look toward heaven and count the stars, if you are able to count them." Then he said to him, "So shall your descendants be." 6 And he believed the Lord, and the Lord[b] reckoned it to him as righteousness.

Reflecting on when my children were little, it's true that family vacations often put our

patience to the test, but looking back, nothing matched the wonder and the magic of a classic road trip. The whole house seemed to buzz with excitement. Laughter bouncing down the hallway. Little feet racing from room to room. Suitcases overflowing with favorite toys. And that frantic, last-minute scramble to find that one special blanket that no one wanted to leave behind. It was those simple, yet chaotic moments, that made our memories unforgettable and filled our journey with love.

I'm not a fan of night driving but back then, it was part of the family routine. My wife and I would give the children baths, slip them into their PJs, and tuck them into bed. Then about three or four o'clock in the morning, with the car packed and ready to go, and while the rest of the world was wrapped in the darkness of the night, we would gently pile everyone in the car and off we would go. With the city lights dissolving behind us and quiet music playing through the speakers, there was a rare peace. Yet, no matter how peaceful the beginning of a trip would be, when everyone woke up, with our destination still far from sight, a small voice would ask a question that would inevitably get on my nerves. You already know what the question is. "Are we there yet?" And my answer would inevitably be the same as a lot of parents out there would say, "We are there when I stop this car and say that we are there."

While funny now, I have come to understand that the question wasn't just a question about mileage or maps. It was a cry born out of boredom and impatience. A small declaration of frustration that said: *"I'm tired of being here. I don't know what's going on and I don't know what's happening. I just want to get to the place that you promised."*

And so often in life, this question becomes the soundtrack of our faith story. God gives us a glimpse, a vision of our lives but when we don't see it happening how we imagine it or when the journey feels longer and the road tougher than expected, we begin to question the promise and the promise maker. Yet, one of the things that you will discover about God is: **God has a destiny for you, a purpose for you, and a plan for you. Yet, God will do it for His reasons, in His way and on His timing.** Said another way, the journey might not look like what you pictured, and the pace might not match your watch, but the promise is still good, and God's timing is always perfect.

This truth is what draws us to Genesis Chapter 15. We eavesdrop on Abram's most vulnerable prayers at the moment where he's asking God: *"I don't know what you're doing. You made me a promise, but you're not in a hurry and I'm starting to struggle with the wait and the uncertainty."*

Genesis Chapter 15 starts with these comforting words: *"After these things the word of the Lord came to Abram in a vision, "Do not be afraid..."* Now before we read too quickly, slow down with Abram for a moment. And sit with him in the ache of delayed fulfilment and the long pause between God's word and its reality.

What many miss is just how long Abram had been waiting. The unfulfilled promise God handed Abram wasn't new. It was stamped with a date a full decade earlier. Imagine you are in college now. The promise was given to Abram when you were learning your multiplication tables in elementary. If you are in your 40s, the promise was given to Abram when you were in your 30s. **Ten years. Three thousand six hundred and fifty sunsets. A decade is a long time when hope is on hold.** Yet, it was ten years ago that God showed up in Abram's life and said to him: *"I'm going to begin to do work in you. This work is not only going to be a blessing to you, but this work is also going to be a blessing to the whole world. Through you Abram, I'm going to make my name great. I'm going to bless you more than you could ever think or imagine. I'm going to give you the Promised Land and through you and your offspring, I'm going to begin a redemptive process that will reconcile my creation back to me once again."*

That is the good news. Yet, here is the problem. Abram gets this promise when he's seventy-five years old. Ten years, a whole decade has passed, and nothing has happened. He has left all that he has known. Every comfort, every memory, every street he had ever called home and still nothing has happened. He finds himself in a foreign land. Each sunrise reminds him that he is a stranger here, but still nothing has happened. He looks over at his wife Sarai and while she is still fine to him, and she still holds his heart, she is not getting any younger and time is fading the hope of children. Two years. Three years. Five years. Seven years. Ten years have passed, and every birthday candle, every season, whispers the same truth. They still have no children.

Is there any wonder that Abram starts wrestling out loud with God? *"God, what are you doing? I keep waiting. I keep hoping. I keep believing. I keep dreaming but I don't see it happening. How many times can I play, Beyonce, "Love on Top?" How many times can we slow drag to John Legend's, "All of Me"?"* But still nothing happened. How many songs, how many silent nights, before faith starts to sound like disappointment?

Notice the tension in the text. Chapter 15 doesn't open with triumphs but begins with the words, *"After these things..."* After these things means that Abram went through some stuff. "After these things..." means that he survived a famine, and a crisis. He had felt the gnaw of hunger in his own belly and the eyes of his family looking to him for hope. He had wrestled with family struggles and marriage separation. And between Chapters 12 and 13 chaos reigned in his life and then you get to Genesis 14. And Genesis 14 brought more drama for Abram. Wars and rescues and heartbreak and fear and anxiety.

The story of Genesis 14 goes that there was a coalition of four kings that decide to raid the land that was supposed to belong to Abram. They invade the land and capture prisoners and bring them back to their land. So, they have all the resources, and all the money and all the people, including Abram's nephew Lot. So, Abraham says by faith, *"I have to go and rescue Lot."*

At eighty-five years old, Abram is no young man. Yet, he goes off to war, to fight a king that just demolished every other king in the area Abram's living. War is a young man's game, yet the Bible says Abram gets the victory. Eighty-five years old and still winning. And after the defeat of his enemy, King Melchizedek blesses him with the spoils of war. Now, Abram finds himself surrounded by wealth. He has a ton of money. He has people. He has power. He has prestige. And I think, in his mind, Abram begins to say to himself: *"Now is the time that the promise will be fulfilled. I've got the money. I've got the people, and I've got the land. Now I control my own destiny."*

But the story takes a turn. After giving a tithe to King Melchizedek, the king of Sodom says to Abram, *"Give me the people but take the goods for yourself."*[62] Yet in an incredible statement of faith, Abram replies:
22 But Abram said to the king of Sodom, "With raised hand I have sworn an oath to the Lord, God Most High, Creator of heaven and earth, 23 that I will

accept nothing belonging to you, not even a thread or the strap of a sandal, so that you will never be able to say, 'I made Abram rich.' [24] *I will accept nothing but what my men have eaten and the share that belongs to the men who went with me—to Aner, Eshkol and Mamre. Let them have their share."*[63]

Say this out loud with me: **God has a plan for my life; and I'm going to trust God.**

And with that declaration made, something happens between the end of chapter 14 and the beginning of Chapter 15. The bible says Abram goes back to his tent and looks at the places where the promises should have taken root, and I believe he starts to wonder. *"Did I make the right choice? God, I keep trying to do it your way, yet nothing is happening. Did I blow it? I had all the power. I had all the money. I could have taken the promises my way. Did I just make a colossal mistake? Because according to the world, this was crazy. No one does this. No one gives up money or power or influence. Could I have forced your promises into reality if I just took things into my own hands?"*

The world says what Abram did was absurd. Who in their right mind gives up a fortune and a seat at the power table? Nobody. Nobody willingly walks away from influence and security. Nobody walks away from success for a promise, right? So there sits Abram, glancing at Sarai, haunted by the slow tick of time, the

156

ache of age, and the piercing silence of dreams deferred. His only prayer, "Are we there yet, God?"

But here, the beauty of God's mercy shines. The bible says the Lord shows up again. And the Lord says to Abram: *"Do not be afraid, Abram, I am your shield; your reward shall be very great."*[64] It's a gentle reminder: Abram, you didn't make a mistake. You are not lost. You are seen. For the first time, God makes the promise very personal. God doesn't look at Abram and say, "What are you doing?" God looks at him and gives him a promise. *"Abram, I am your shield. I am your great reward. I'm going to protect you. I'm going to watch over you. I'm going to be with you. I have a plan, and My hand is moving even when you can't see it."*

This is what I love about God. God appears, not to condemn, but to gently open our eyes, to show us there is more waiting that can be measured by what we see. Maybe this is your story. God gave you a vision to leave debt behind and to walk in financial freedom. You heard of this concept called, "10-10-80" God's plan for your money. The principle is for every dollar that you have, you tithe the first 10 percent, you save and invest the second 10 percent, and then you ask God how to manage the remaining 80 percent. It's working. You see progress. Then, out of nowhere, the car breaks down. An unexpected bill snatches away what felt like a breakthrough. And suddenly you are worse off than when you started and you cry out to God, "Where are you now?"

Here's the truth I've learned about God: **don't mistake God's silence for God's absence**. Sometimes God waits until our strength is gone to show us that His strength is enough. He is the kind of God that doesn't show up just to fix things. He shows up to grow our faith. When your questions outnumber your answers and when your hope is running low, that's the moment that God opens your eyes to see that what He has for you is still worth the wait.

What I like about Abram is that he is not afraid to be honest with God. *"But Abram said, "O, Lord God, what will you give me, for I continue childless, and the heir of my house is Eliezer of Damascus?"*[65] This is not a question of disobedience. This is a question that comes from his heart. And this is what I love about God. **God is never afraid of your questions if you approach Him with a heart that desires to seek Him.**

If I could paraphrase Genesis 15:2, Abram says to God: "I know you are intentional, but I can't see you working. I literally could have died on the battlefield without bearing any children. I'm looking around and nothing is going on that is different. Am I going to have to give all that I have to a servant in my house? Is that your plan God? Is that what you're really trying to do? You said you were going to give me children, but have you looked at me? I am not getting any younger.

Children are for young folks. You said if I tithe, if I serve, if I read your word, if I do right and walk with integrity, if I stop doing things my way, if I have a relationship with you, you would heal me, you would deliver me, you would provide for me, you will bless me, you will reveal your promise to me, but I don't see it happening. Lord, I'm struggling. Can you really do what you promise?"

Can you feel Abram's fear? I don't know about you, but there have been moments in my own life that I have found myself in my own tent looking around for a sign of deliverance or a glimpse of my breakthrough and when seeing nothing asking God, "What are you doing? I can't see it happening."

Here is God's response to Abram's question, *"This man shall not be your heir; no one but your very own issue shall be your heir."*[66] In other words, **when you start to doubt what God can do, remember who God is**. God leans in and says, *"I am your shield. I am your reward.*[67] *I am the great I am. And I will do what I said I was going to do."* Yet, that's not the shout. Verse 5 is what messed me up. In verse 5, God calls Abram to step outside, to break out of the cramped corners of his disappointment and *"Look up at the sky and count the stars—if indeed you can count them." Then he said to him, "So shall your offspring*[d] *be."*

In other words, God's message to Abram: *"What you can't see, I see. What you can't comprehend, I know. I'm not asking you to understand or figure it out. I'm asking you to trust me. When you look at the sky, I am not asking you to count all the stars. I'm asking you to trust the maker of the stars. I'm asking you to trust the one who calls every star by name and who created it before you even existed. I'm asking you to trust in the one who was before there was a was, and will be, when is and was, are no more. I'm asking you to trust the one who speaks light into places where there was darkness. I'm asking you to believe in the one who spun the whole world into orbit and the one who holds gravity itself in His hands. I'm asking you to trust in the one who has wisdom beyond your wisdom and knowledge beyond your knowledge and power beyond your power. I'm asking you to trust in me, Abram."*

And I love the witness and the simplicity of verse 6. It says, *"Abram believed."*

How Trusting God Helps Us Dream Again

Trust in God isn't about shutting down our questions. It's the act of handing our uncertainty to the One whose vision is infinite. When Abram dared to trust God, he was about to imagine a future that defied logic and biology. Trust in God cracks open the door to dreaming again and gives our faith new volume, our hearts new courage and our imaginations fresh fire. Trusting God means allowing hope to become rebellious to facts and figures and it empowers us to reimagine what's possible and to dream dreams that are only limited by God's creativity and not our circumstances. And trusting God allows us to push past the barriers of fear and complacency that sometimes hinders us from achieving the great things that God has in store for us.

Genesis 15:6 records: *⁶Abram believed...* **Has anything changed?** Nothing visible changed. There were no signs, no sudden miracles, no answers yet. But the Bible records a quiet, daring act: *"Abram believed the Lord."* Don't miss the depth of this moment because Abram shows us what faith is. **Faith is not a feeling and it's not an emotion. Faith is a choice that says: even when I can't see it happening, I trust in what God says**.

In that moment, Abram decides, *"God, I don't see it happening. Yet, I choose to trust you. I am not trusting in what I see. I'm trusting in what you say."* And the Bible says that the Lord is so honored by Abram's choice and his display of faith that God gives him the gift of righteousness: setting him right, washing him clean, making him holy, drawing him into intimate relationship, and freeing him from the shackles of shame and guilt. To be righteous means to be holy. To be righteous means to be in right relationship with God. To be righteous means that you are free; not bound by sin and shame.

And this is why Abram's story is so remarkable when you consider who Abram is. He is going to do some wacky things. He is going to mess up and fail and fall short of the glory of God. Yet, God looks at him and says: *"Because of your faith, I'm crediting righteousness to your account and I'm going to give to you what you don't deserve."*

Because Abram dared to choose faith, he stood before God as if he had never failed, as if he had never fallen, as if he was never unfaithful. And in that moment, God declares over his life: *"I'm going to use all my power and all of my love and all of my wisdom and all of my greatness for your good, not just now, but for all eternity. I'm setting my affection upon you and I'm declaring before the world your righteousness. Therefore, no matter what you have done and no matter what you will do, I am your God, and I am for you."* That's how big a deal faith is to God. But don't miss this. Before Abram was declared righteous, Abram had to get outside of his tent and look up. Right where you are, **shout with me: Look up! Look up!**

The Journey is Not a Straight Line

If you listen closely beneath the noise of progress, you will hear a quieter truth humming in Genesis 15: the journey to promise, to purpose, to greatness was never meant to be a straight line. Abram's story is no parade. It's a pilgrimage. By the time we meet him here, he has weathered famine, family drama, moral missteps, stunning rescues, and the long ache of waiting on God.

Years have passed since the first, bold promise. Years marked not just by movement, but by confusion, longing and the kind of questions that keep a person up at night. Yet, through all the sideways steps, and restarts and disappointments, God remains near, providing Abram new directions, steadying what shakes, and guiding what feels lost. Faith, you see, does not travel through straight paths. Often the story of great pursuits, whether spiritual, personal or professional, are marked by zigzags along the way.

The Apple Comeback: Genius in the Zigzags

Consider Apple. Yes, that Apple. The tech giant that sits on top of the world's financial heap. But rewind the tape. In the 1990s, Apple was battered, bruised and nearly bankrupt. The world said it was finished, a relic of tech's precocious past. Executives came and went. Products flopped. Its market share struggled. In those days, it wasn't about innovation, it was about survival. But like Abram in his tent, someone kept looking up and kept seeing possibility hidden in uncertainty. That person was Steve Jobs. Steve Jobs was driven by a fierce, almost stubborn vision that tomorrow could be different. He returned to the company that he founded, not with nostalgia, but with clarity and courage. Jobs and his team had to zigzag. They cut beloved projects and bet everything on new ideas no one understood. The iMac, then the iPod, then the iPhone changed everything. Every step was a climb towards success. Often it was a crawl in the dark. Nevertheless, Apple's renaissance, or should I say breakthrough, was birthed not from steady progress, but from resilience that dared to dream again.

Marvel: A Universe Built on Comebacks

Consider Marvel Studios. Today it is easy to see the billion-dollar movie empire and say, "Oh, what a great success it is with its superheroes and cultural dominance." But Marvel Studio's Road to blockbuster hits was anything but heroic. In the 1990s, Marvel fell into bankruptcy, its characters languishing in obscurity. They hustled for relevance by licensing out icons like Spider-Man and Iron Man just to pay creditors. The story for Marvel seemed closed. Another American legend gone bust. Yet, Marvel's leaders kept looking up, even as the world watched them stumble. They reimagined their future, took creative risks, and dared to dream again. The Marvel Cinematic Universe wasn't born in boardrooms. No, it was forged through unrelenting setbacks and creative comebacks. And today, Marvel stands as a living testament that greatness comes most often through zigzags and second chances.

164

The Weather Channel: Seeing Above the Storm

Just as Abram stood beneath the night skies, unable to count the stars but called to imagine what God could do, John Coleman dared to "look up" beyond what was visible. John Coleman, a respected meteorologist, dreamt of a network that would broadcast the weather every hour of every day. When he pitched the idea, critics rejected it. No one believed that people would tune in just to watch reports on the weather. Even his colleagues wondered out loud if he had lost it.

Yet, Coleman kept dreaming, kept pressing forward fueled by one simple conviction: weather impacts every person, every day. With the help of Frank Batten and Landmark Communications, he founded the Weather Channel in 1980. Insiders doubted a national audience existed for such a niche idea. But the channel caught on and by the end of the decade, The Weather Channel was in nearly every American home. What once seemed trivial became indispensable and changed culture in unexpected ways.

Peloton: Reimagining the Possible

John Foley, a former Barnes & Noble executive and fitness enthusiast, loved boutique studio workouts, but couldn't find time for them in his busy life. Foley dreamed of blending technology with the energy and community of live, group workouts, delivered directly to people's homes. The idea? A high-end stationary bike paired with immersive, streamed fitness classes led by charismatic instructors.

Foley's idea was met with much skepticism and a ton of rejections. Investors told him that fitness hardware was a loser. Others insisted that no one would pay thousands of dollars for a bike and a $39/month subscription to exercise at home. But Foley refused to surrender to doubt. He built his team. Opened a showroom in New York City and persuaded a few believers to invest. Peloton's growth was slow at first, but once people tried it, they became the brand's fiercest advocates. Everyone had reasons to say no, but Foley had as many reasons as possible to say yes.

During the pandemic, Peloton's popularity soared. People around the world formed digital communities, rode together, laughed together, sweated together, all while the world was locked down. What was once "crazy" became mainstream, and fitness instructors you never heard of before became celebrities and social media stars. Foley's dream, doubted by so many, ended up revolutionizing an entire industry.

When you weave the journeys of Apple, Marvel, the Weather Channel and Peloton into Abram's story, you discover something profound. Just as Abram looked up, hesitant and hopeful, unsure and unyielding, these companies remind us that destiny often emerges on winding roads. Sometimes you must lose your way before you find your purpose. And **sometimes greatness is not in the climb, but in the courage to start again, to adapt, to reimagine, to look up even when the night is dark and the stars seem out of reach.** Yet, it's in the reimagining and in the dreaming that you discover that the bends and twists and double backs of the journey are not failures. In fact, it's faith and not defeat. And it represents another star that God calls us to count, and another night that God calls us to trust that what is ahead of us will make sense to us someday, if we keep moving forward and keep looking up.

Back to our story...

So often God makes us a promise. *"I am your shield which means I'll protect you. I am your great reward which means joy and hope and peace and blessing is found in relationship with me. I am for you; all you must do is come and believe and trust me."* Yet so often we miss seeing the promises of God come true, not because of God's silence, but because we are stuck in our tents. Stuck in our tents of fear and confusion and doubts and second-guessing. Stuck in our tents focused on what we see and how we feel and what we see and how we feel and what we see and how we feel, to the point that our perceptions become our reality. As a result, we start thinking that nothing is happening, that nothing is getting better, that what we see today defines what God can do tomorrow.

So, God does something extraordinary. God pulls us out of our tent, out of our situation, out of our anxiety and our narrow view and commands us to, *"Look up! You can't count all the stars in the sky, but I am still a promise keeper. I know it has taken longer than you expected but do you think I'm done? Look up! What you can see doesn't define what I can do in your life. Do you really think your problems are freaking me out? Look up! I am still Jehovah Jireh, your provider. Do you really think that I can't handle what you're going through right now? Look up! If I be for you, who can be against you? Do you think this is the first time anyone struggled with what you are struggling with? Look up! What the enemy meant for evil, I will use it for your good."*

I don't know who needs to hear this but time and time again, God has proven He will do just what He said He would do. That's the majesty and the power of the cross. Jesus said: If I be lifted up, I will draw all people to myself. And He said: The thief comes to steal and destroy but I've come that you might have life and have it more abundantly. Yet, there were those who didn't see it happening.

Jesus said: I am the light of the world. I am the bread of life. I am the door. I am the good shepherd. I am the resurrection and the life. I am the vine. And even though the storms may come, I will still bless you. *Yet, there were those who didn't see it happening.*

So, on a hill called Calvary, Jesus hung his head and died. His enemies laughed, yet they didn't see it happening. The grave thought it had won, yet it didn't see it happening. Though darkness covered the earth, it didn't see it happening. When Pilate sealed the tomb, he didn't see it happening. The devil rejoiced, yet he didn't see it happening. Pestilence and sickness and shame high-fived one another, yet they didn't see it happening. Because with his death, our debt was paid, and we were redeemed. And early one Sunday morning, Jesus rose just like he said he would.

I know you are struggling. I know it feels like the vision that God has for your life is fading. I know it seems like the promise is fleeting. Yet can I encourage you? Put your faith in Jesus, our anchor and hope, because He will never let you down. Because even when we don't see it happening, remember we serve a promise keeper. And in God's time and in God's way, God will do what God said He would do.

CHAPTER 9

What's in a Name?

Genesis 17:1-8
The Sign of the Covenant

17 When Abram was ninety-nine years old, the Lord appeared to Abram and said to him, "I am God Almighty;₍ᵃ₎ walk before me, and be blameless. ² And I will make my covenant between me and you and will make you exceedingly numerous." ³ Then Abram fell on his face, and God said to him, ⁴ "As for me, this is my covenant with you: You shall be the ancestor of a multitude of nations. ⁵ No longer shall your name be Abram,₍ᵇ₎ but your name shall be Abraham,₍ᶜ₎ for I have made you the ancestor of a multitude of nations. ⁶ I will make you exceedingly fruitful, and I will make nations of you, and kings shall come from you. ⁷ I will establish my covenant between me and you and your offspring after you throughout their generations, for an everlasting covenant, to be God to you and to your offspring after you. ⁸ And I will give to you and to your offspring after you the land where you are now an alien, all the land of Canaan, for a perpetual holding, and I will be their God."

Abram's story reveals that sometimes the greatest shifts come before circumstances change. For years, Abram lived with unfulfilled hopes and the aches of barrenness. Yet, before Isaac was born, the promised son of Abraham and Sarah,[68] God changed Abram's name to Abraham, inviting him into a future he could hardly imagine. And by doing so, God did not merely give Abram a new identity, he reframed Abram's reality by speaking possibility over his limitations.

I remember sitting in the back pew of my home church as a child, watching my father preach about a God who specializes in making ways when there seems to be no way. I wore the "preacher's kid" label with all of its weight, sometimes an honor, sometimes a burden, but always a reminder. Alongside it came others like "not enough," "just ordinary," and "nothing special." There were seasons when those labels boxed me in, when expectations pressed down hard and hope felt distant.

But God is notorious for giving new names before any miracles appear. He called Abram "father of many" when Abram couldn't see a child anywhere in his future. That's the power of Genesis 17. God's promise arrives ahead of the evidence, and destiny is spoken into places that seem impossibly dry. Yet it was in those quiet moments with God that I found a new whisper: *"Before I change what's around you, let me change what's inside you."* And like Abram, my journey shifted not when my circumstances did, but when I allowed God to speak new life, and new names, over my story.

Gradually, the labels lost their grip. Instead of "just ordinary," I began to hear "builder," and "visionary," and "shepherd." And out of the shadow of "preacher's kid," I discovered a courage that was mine and not inherited but divinely spoken. And I learned that every "no" was another invitation for faith. And breakthroughs happen not when everything looks perfect, but when I dare to see myself through the lens of God's promises.

The Power of Reimagining

Consider Abram, a man of ninety-five years young, carrying the name "exalted father." I think about the weight of that name. Every time someone called "Abram" it was a subtle reminder of promises yet to be fulfilled, dreams still waiting, hopes on pause. Maybe you know what it is like to walk with labels that announce possibility but remind you more of what hasn't happened than what has happened.

Genesis 17 offers something remarkable. God steps into Abram's weary story, announcing himself as "El Shaddai," the God who isn't just present, but more than enough for every need, and every ache and unspoken request. And before there's any evidence of change, long before a single prayer is answered the way Abram hoped, or any visible sign that the old promises were finally about to break through, God interrupts the silence with a new name.

Abram falls to his face as an act of surrender, maybe even exhaustion, and God begins to speak new vision into an old situation: *4 "As for me, this is my covenant with you: You shall be the ancestor of a multitude of nations. 5 No longer shall your name be Abram,[b] but your name shall be Abraham,[c] for I have made you the ancestor of a multitude of nations."*[69]

This blesses me because it's a reminder that God doesn't wait for proof. God doesn't check his credentials or ask for a resume. Instead, in the middle of Abram's limitations, while the ache and emptiness of unanswered prayers are still real, God speaks possibility into his life. God looks at his barren places and sees the blueprint for abundance. God isn't fazed by empty seasons. God sees beyond every "not yet," every history of pain, every door that's seemingly slammed shut. And instead of walking away, God invites Abram, and subsequently invites you and me, into a new covenant relationship designed to outlast and outshine anything that came before. That's what your God and our God can do.

That's the mystery and **the beauty of God's economy. Hope is declared before fruit ever appears.** That's good. Let me say that again. Hope is declared before fruit ever appears. Think about that. God doesn't wait for us to qualify. God doesn't check our spiritual resume or measure us by our perfect attendance. God speaks potential right into our brokenness. God calls us while we are still confused and still asking why the last chapter feels unfinished and the old promises look expired.

Maybe that's where you are right now with God. "God, you promised me something five years ago. Where is it? Was my faithfulness wasted? Have my prayers and my tears been in vain?" It's a fair question. But here's the revelation that I hope will bless you like it blessed me: **God's promise for your life is never static or one dimensional.** God is not a check the box kind of person or someone locked in the past. So, if life shifted, if doors closed, if the answer looks different than you once expected. It's just a sign that God is still creating and is still curating a vision for you that isn't trapped in a single moment, or a lost opportunity, or even a past disappointment.

So why do we stay stuck? Why do we mourn what is lesser or miss what's over, when God is still speaking or revealing to us something greater and something better? Could it be that we are holding onto something God has already outgrown? Or that we can't lift our eyes high enough to see the new beginning God is inviting us into? God changing Abram's name to Abraham is proof that God's dynamic and creative power is never just behind you. It's possibly right in front of you, even if it looks different than you planned.

That's the amazing thing about a creative God. God's vision for your life is not anchored to one season or one circumstance. Halleluiah! Instead, God's vision for our lives is big enough to start over, strong enough to restore what's lost, and dynamic enough to bring forth what's missing with something entirely brand new. God's word is active and alive and moving. And when God reimagines your life, resurrection and new beginnings are always possible, no matter what the past tried to define. God's promises for you are still unfolding, even when the script looks different than you had planned.

Breaking Free from Limiting Labels

The change of Abram's name to Abraham was about far more than linguistical esthetics. It denoted a divine shift, a spiritual upgrade that aligned Abram with the promises and purposes of God for his life. "Abraham" means "father of many," which must have sounded ridiculous to some when considering he only had one child at the time of Genesis 17 and both he and Sarah were well past their prime. But God's focus wasn't on what Abraham lacked. It was on the future God was unfolding. Scripture is rich with moments where God rewrites a person's future by giving them a new name: Jacob's transformation into Israel, Simon's redefinition as Peter, Saul's dramatic conversion into Paul, and even Sarai being renamed Sarah, "princess" and "mother of nations." These are not random changes or accidental edits. They are divine invitations to step into greater callings and new destinies and visions bigger and larger than those scripted in the past.

Labels are not just ancient history. They shape our modern lives too. Whether it's "too old," or "not qualified," or "single parent," or "former addict," or "not enough," these words cling to us like a coat that we can't unzip. I'm reminded of a man who struggled with homelessness and haunted for years by the label of "failure" by his family. Then one day a friend spoke new truth over his life. He said to him, "You are not a failure, and you are not forsaken. You are capable and you are redeemed." At first the declaration sounded like just hollow words. But in time, the man dared to fill out a job application. Then he saved and saved and before long he became a homeowner. And in time, redemption rewrote this man's story where limitation once held him back.

How we see ourselves influences every move we make. If we wear the name "broken," we begin to move through life cautiously, expecting to crack. But when God speaks a new name, God calls us above and beyond the boundaries of those old labels, inviting us to move and to act and to dream with a courage we didn't know we had.

Your New You Starts Today

Let me tell you, **when God changes your name, it's deeper than cosmetic surgery. It's a shift in the whole trajectory of your life.** The new name isn't just a badge to wear. It's the Lord's invitation to leave behind every label, every generational curse, every narrative that tries to keep you in a box. When God renames you, God is saying, "Step forward. Because I've destined you for more than what you were."

This principle is not just biblical, it shows up in history, and business and entertainment. Think about Muhammad Ali, who cast off Cassius Clay, a name he called a "slave name," to embrace a new identity and purpose. Think about Malcolm X, who dropped a name stolen by history and claimed his "X" as a stand for self-determination. Think about Mark Twain, born Samuel Langhorne Clemens, who swapped his riverboat past for a pen name that gave birth to one of America's literary legends. Think about Elton John, who rebranded himself from Reginald Dwight, in order to unleash a new stage presence and artistic expression that was living within him. Think about Lady Gaga, who changed her name from Stefani Germanotta, crafting a musical persona that allowed her to break musical boundaries and connect with fans as a symbol of artistic freedom and self-expression. And think about Beyonce, who created an alter ego that she named "Sasha Fierce." Sasha Fierce was not just a stage name but a calculated persona that empowered Beyonce to express a dimension of her personality that she might have kept hidden. Each name change, each moment, a step away from being boxed in, and a leap toward the future they felt compelled to create.

Think about Oprah, for example. Born Orpah after a biblical figure. Yet a simple misspelling on her birth certificate and a lifetime of mispronunciations rebranded her for the world. "Oprah" became not just a new sound, but a symbol of overcoming poverty and trauma and countless obstacles. The one letter difference launched a unique global icon who would change lives and redefine what's possible.

Think about Facebook changing its name to Meta to reflect a broader vision beyond social media. And don't forget the story of Dunkin.' For nearly 70 years, "Americans lined up for Dunkin' Donuts." But as the brand grew, it realized its future wasn't in what was familiar. Its future was in something new. So, it did the unthinkable. After 70 years of success and expansion, Dunkin' Donuts changed its name to Dunkin,' not forgetting its past but opening the door to a broader mission focused on innovation for a new generation. They invested in new technology and implemented new processes but kept the playful pink and orange branding to unite their heritage with a renewed vision for the future. Showing that sometimes, embracing a new name is about unlocking what comes next. But here is the good news. Your new day starts today.

This renaming, this rebranding, this dreaming is not just for icons or companies. This is for you! If you are going to walk in your new name, I have some principles that I believe will help you:

1. **Call out the labels that have limited you.** What names, what judgments, what narratives have held you back? Who spoke those words over you? Was it your family, bosses, even yourself? Write them down. Now ask yourself, are they true by God's standards, or have they just been true so far?

2. **Embrace God's definition.** What does Scripture really say about you? What would it look like to let God's voice speak louder than your history or your critics? Remind yourself what God calls you, like *blessed, loved, and redeemed* and post these truths where you can see them daily.

3. **Speak your name daily, even before there's evidence.** This isn't about pretending or faking it until you make it, it's about a faith that speaks what God has promised. Establish a daily habit of declaring God's truth over your

life, affirming who you are in Jesus Christ and what He says about your future.

4. **Take new steps.** Let your new identity move you. What bold decisions would you make if God's name for you was already true? Who would you reach out to, what doors would you knock on, what boundaries would you dare break? Is it time to apply for that new job, or start that business, or mend a relationship, or dream beyond the old horizons?

Let your new name be your rallying cry and let your new name be your step forward toward chasing bigger dreams and overcoming old boundaries.

What's in a Name? Everything.

What's in a name? Everything. Names mark milestones, they define the chapters, and they set the tone for each new season of your story. As for me, I can still hear my mother opening the back sliding door, and yelling, *"Alex! Dinner is ready!"* Her voice echoing in the dusk of a summer's evening as the sun set behind the Georgia pines. Back then, I was simply Alex, the preacher's kid, the smart yet awkward country boy from Midway, Georgia. That name felt familiar and safe, but it also felt unfinished and uncomfortable, like wearing a coat a size too small. There was something bigger waiting beneath the surface, something that small-town Georgia had not yet seen.

Then came that first day of sixth grade. My heart pounded in my chest. My fingers trembled as I clutched the straps of my backpack and walked through the narrow halls of Sandy Run School, the small and only private school in Liberty County, Georgia. The classroom was thick with anticipation, and the smell of chalk dust and the shuffling of ten awkward eleven and twelve year old feet. Ms. Strickland, my teacher with kind eyes, called roll and paused at my name. As the sunlight sliced between the slatted blinds, I felt every eye settle on me as she called my name, "Is Alex Maxell here?"

Without any hesitation, I responded, "My name is no longer Alex Maxell. My name is Charles Alexander Maxell, Jr." My voice barely above a whisper yet it rang with a new strength that surprised even me. In that hush, I claimed a name that was both mine and my father's, a legacy that felt heavy across my shoulders and thrilling in my spirit. And for one beautiful moment, everything was possible.

But not every name came easily. Some seasons, the new labels felt like clothes borrowed from someone stronger, hanging loose and unfamiliar. I swallowed fear as I tried on "leader." And I fought self-doubt as I stepped into "reverend." Other names like "worthy" and "enough" took years for me to grow into their truth.

And yes, there were seasons that I wore names that pierced my spirit like "failure," "outsider," "too much" or "not enough." Some days these names felt more real than any promise God had spoken. And there were moments I found myself wondering out loud if these names would define me more than God's voice ever could.

Yet, here is what I discovered through every chapter of growth and struggle. The good names were not just who I was becoming. They were who I always was in God's eyes. And those painful names? They were never permanent, and they were never more powerful than God's purpose. In fact, the very failures I thought disqualified me, became the foundation for the ministry that God was building through me.

Yet, above all, it was the name "Daddy" that changed me in ways I never imagined. I can still see Madison, my firstborn child, wobbling across the living room on unsteady legs, her face lighting up with pure triumph as she took her very first step into my waiting arms. I think of my son, Charles III, every time I catch that determined look in his eyes, or see our shared name proudly stitched on the back of his college football jersey. And my heart swelled with pride watching my youngest daughter, Skylar, standing before a crowd of hundreds, her voice steady and passionate, as she delivered an unforgettable speech on the inequalities in our education system.

Watching my wife light up every space she enters, witnessing my children flourish through their own seasons, I am constantly reminded how God's faithfulness spills over in every corner of our lives. With each new name, thankfulness swells in my chest, sometimes spilling out in tears, but never born of regret. Day by day, I see how God refused to leave me limited to the insecurities of my childhood. Instead, through every transformation, from Alex to Charles, from son to father, from preacher's kid to pastor, from boyfriend to husband, God stretched my possibilities far beyond what I could ever imagine.

This journey isn't mine alone. As I look back, I realize God's habit of renaming didn't end with ancient stories, it's alive in us today. In Scripture, God changed Abram to Abraham, Jacob to Israel, Saul to Paul, a divine reminder that identity is not fixed but formed in purpose. Yet, the greatest name change belongs to Jesus Himself. Paul records his transformation this way: *"9 Therefore God exalted him even more highly and gave him the name that is above every other name, 10 so that at the name given to Jesus every knee should bend, in heaven and on earth and under the earth, 11 and every tongue should confess that Jesus Christ is Lord, to the glory of God the Father."70*

So, let me ask you right now: What name is God whispering to your heart? What future is waiting for you to claim it? Maybe God's new name for you is business owner, college graduate, leader, healer or advocate. Or maybe your new name is builder, scholar, winner, executive, or entrepreneur. Or maybe it's something that sounds like teacher, mentor, parent, friend, coach, comforter, or encourager. Whatever the name is, it is waiting for you to embrace it.

Here's the thing, every day you spend answering to labels that don't belong to you like "failure," or "too late" or "not enough" or "washed up" or "forgotten," is a day you waste your power. But that's not your story. That's never been your story.

What if today you laid down every name this world pressed on you that does not fit your calling? What if you dared to dream again, to answer to the name God is giving you? The name pulsing with His promise. The name rooted in His vision for your life.

What are you waiting for? Your real life, your real name is waiting. And it starts when you say yes to who God says you are.

CHAPTER 10
Conclusion: It's Up to You Now

If you've made it this far, congratulations! But you're not done. You're here because you want to change your life. And I'm telling you right now: you can. Not next year. Not when you feel "ready." You can change your life starting today.

From the very first page, I asked you to remember what it felt like to dream as a child, when your imagination knew no bounds and hope stretched as far as you could see. Like you, I've known what it means to have those dreams interrupted by disappointment, by loss, by the slow drift into the "good enough" of Haran. I wrote this book standing at my own crossroads, wrestling with the tension between comfort and calling, between the safety of the familiar and the promise of something greater. I wrote this book because I needed to remind myself and you that **it's possible to dream again, no matter where you are on your journey.**

Looking back, I realize how many times I've settled for "good enough." There were seasons when fear disguised itself as wisdom, convincing me to stay put rather than risk the unknown. I remember the ache of dreams deferred, the quiet resignation that crept in when hope seemed too costly. But beneath that resignation, there was always a restless whisper, a reminder that I was made for more. Sometimes, that whisper felt like a burden. Other times, it was a lifeline.

Writing these words, I am reminded of the nights I lay awake, heart pounding with excitement and dread, wondering if I was foolish to want more. I have felt the sting of failure, the embarrassment of starting over, and the vulnerability of admitting I was lost. But I have also tasted the sweetness of small victories, the quiet pride of taking just one brave step forward, even when the outcome was uncertain. If I could speak to my younger self, I would say: **Don't let fear masquerade as wisdom. And don't let comfort become your cage.** The longing you feel isn't weakness. It's the compass pointing you home.

Here's the truth: most people settle in their own personal Haran. They get comfortable. They let fear, routine, or the opinions of others talk them out of chasing what they really want. They let their dreams collect dust. **But you? You're not like most people.** You picked up this book because something inside you was restless. You know there's more. You know you're meant for Canaan, not Haran.

Abram's journey wasn't flawless, far from it. He made mistakes, doubted, and even needed God to remind him of the dream more than once. God changed his name from Abram to Abraham as a sign of a new identity and a renewed promise. But here's what's unforgettable: despite the setbacks, the detours, and the moments of uncertainty, Abram never went back to Haran. Why? Because Haran was never meant to be his home. And it's not meant to be yours, either.

Haran represents the halfway point, the place where it's easy to settle for comfort, familiarity, of "good enough." It's where dreams can quietly fade if you let them. But God's call in Abram's life was always about moving forward, not looking back. Even when Abram faltered, God kept calling him onward, reminding him of the promise, inviting him to believe again, to risk again, to step out in faith even when the path wasn't clear.

That's the call for you, too. You may have made mistakes. You may have lost sight of your dream or needed reminders along the way. But don't let that convince you to turn around or settle in your own Haran. The comfort zone, the place of "almost," is not your final destination. God's promise is ahead, not behind. The life you're called to live, the life that sets your soul on fire is still waiting for you, just beyond your comfort zone.

I've learned that growth is rarely comfortable. It's messy, unpredictable, and often lonely. You may have lost sight of your dream or settled for reminders along the way. But don't let that convince you to turn back. Every detour, every setback, every moment in the "in between place" of "almost" has shaped you. God's promise is real and not behind. The life you're called to live, the one that sets your soul on fire, is still waiting for you, just beyond your comfort zone.

What I've Learned:

- **Faith over fear:** choosing to trust God's vision, even when the road ahead is hidden in fog.

- **Perseverance through setbacks:** knowing that dreams are often realized on the other side of hardship.

- **Hope and restoration:** believing that empty spaces can become places of hope, and that God can restore what was lost.

- **Purpose beyond self:** discovering that your dreams are meant not just for you, but to bless others.

So, here's what you need to do right now:

- **Stop waiting for permission.** You don't need anyone's approval to go after what sets your soul on fire. Not your parents, not your boss, not your friends. The only permission slip you need is the one you write for yourself.

- **Get honest about where you've settled.** Where in your life are you playing small? Where are you letting comfort win over courage? Write it down. Call it out.

- **Decide what you want.** Not what you think you "should" want. What do you actually want? Get specific. Vague dreams get vague results.

- **Surround yourself with lifters, not leeches.** Find people who push you, challenge you, and celebrate your wins. Let go of those who pull you back to Haran.

*And let me say this from my heart. **I am so proud of you. I'm proud of me. I'm proud of us for wanting more, for not settling, for daring to dream again.***

I believe in you! That's why I wrote this book. Not just to share my story, but because I know what it's like to wrestle with disappointment, to stand at the crossroads, to wonder if it's too late or if you're too far gone. I wrote this book because I needed to remind myself, and you, that it's possible to dream again, no matter where you are on your journey.

So, as we close this book, I hope you feel seen. I hope you feel understood. And most of all, I hope you feel empowered to step out of your own Haran, carrying both the lessons of your past and the hope for your future. The journey is yours. The choice is yours. And you are not alone. Haran was never meant to be your home. The life God has for you is always larger than the life you're living now. So, step out and **dare to dream again!**

Acknowledgements

I never used to do this, but since starting this book, I now always turn to the Acknowledgments first whenever I pick up a new book. I do this because I'm curious about people behind the scenes – the cast and crew who bring the story to life. Writing this book has only deepened my appreciation for the power of teamwork.

If you're reading this, please know how profoundly grateful I am for the extraordinary circle of love and support that has surrounded me throughout this journey. While some people are fortunate to have a team, I am blessed with a village: remarkable people who inspire me, love me unconditionally, and never let me settle for less than my purpose. To God, and all of you, thank you for being my foundation and my inspiration.

First and foremost, I want to thank my wife, Rev. Dr. Jennifer Watley Maxell. Your belief in my dreams, even when I doubted them, carried me through the Haran years. I didn't think it would take this long to put idea to pen, but here we are! I know...what took me so long? Your pep talks (and occasional tough but needed reality checks) kept me grounded and moving forward. I am forever grateful for your love, belief in me, and your uncanny ability to remind me that this book wouldn't write itself.

When folks asked me what it means to be blessed, the faces of my children come to mind. To Madison Savannah Maxell, Charles A. Maxell, III, and Skylar Elise Maxell: you are my greatest motivation and the reason I strive to become better every day. I know you thought I was just goofing off in the office all those days. But now you see, there was a method to my madness. Seriously, I hope my work inspires you to reach for all that God has for you, to never stop dreaming, never stop becoming, and to occasionally feed the dogs.

If you are lucky in life, God will bless you with one amazing mother. Well, God blessed me with three. To the mothers who did not give me life but have given me so much love, Ophelia Maxell and Muriel Watley, your kindness has shaped me in ways words cannot express. Thank you for pretending not to notice when I raided your snacks and left evidence of my crimes.

To my sisters, Carlynda Maxell, Major, USAF (Ret.), and Dr. Carmela Maxell, and my nephews, Vincent-Charles Taijeron Finona, George Vaughn Martin III, Logan Charles Harrison, and my niece, Noemi Aleah Runyan, thank you for your steadfast support and for always cheering me on. And no, you can't have any of the royalties. It's for my retirement, or a really nice dinner. Just kidding. I love you!

A heartfelt thank you to Rev. Dr. William Watley for graciously writing the Foreword. Not only do I call you Dad (father-in-law) and pastor, but I also credit you for teaching me that the reason that a person gets up at 5AM to write is because secretly they really are praying it will help them go back to sleep. Well Dad, it hasn't worked. But I do find that I do my best work at 5AM in the morning.

Many family members and friends have poured into me through the years and helped me get to this point: Daisey Pray, Shonda Brownlee, Derrick Pray, Natheniel Pray, Larry Shaw, Matthew Watley, Shawna Watley, Alexanderia Watley, Marian Watley, Carlton Gibson, Bennett Wyche, Robert James II, Kenneth Rance, Gerald Cooke, Robert Grant, Lajuanda Johnson, Helaina Jolly, Sou Ford, LaVonda McLean, Sam Spaulding, Rick Williams, Charles Marable, Caroline Christmas, Edsel Robinson, Tomaree Tarpley, Leaticia Roberts, Brian Lunceford, Renee Lunceford, Kelly Williams, Diana Lavender Woodruff, Nicholas Woodruff, Takia Lamb, and Cheryl Brown Baker. Your encouragement is only matched by your patience in listening to my brilliant (and not-so-brilliant) brainstorms. Thank you for your edits to this manuscript, for urging me to dream bigger, for lifting me up when I faltered, and for making sure I never gave up. Your faith in me has made all the difference. Drinks are on me (but only if you buy the next round).

As for the book itself, I am grateful to Adam Mixon, my editor and friend. Your insight, patience, and encouragement have been invaluable. I could not have brought this book to life without your partnership. I appreciate you, my brother. And I promise it won't take me this long in the future to believe in what you say.

Finally, to my church family, The Breakthrough Fellowship, to my Macedonia Ministry Cohort, and to the 2020 Class of Leadership Atlanta, and every person who has walked beside me, offered a kind word, or simply inspired me along the way, this book is as much yours as it is mine. Thank you, from the depths of my heart, and for helping me reach my own Promised Land – one awkward preacher saying at a time.

About the Author

Charles Maxell, Jr. is a highly accomplished executive with over 30 years of experience driving growth and innovation for leading insurance and professional services firms, including CNA Insurance, Zurich Insurance, Willis Towers Watson, Aon, Marsh and the Baldwin Group. With expertise in leveraging technology, creativity, and data analytics, Charles has consistently delivered double-digit revenue growth while addressing complex challenges in dynamic business environments. His strategic vision and relentless focus on results have established him as a trusted leader in competitive markets worldwide.

Renowned for his ability to turn vision into action, Charles has spearheaded transformative initiatives that have redefined business success. At Zurich and Aon, he led the turnaround of underperforming business units, within just 18 months. As an influential change agent, Charles excels at crafting innovative, brand-building strategies that empower teams to exceed expectations while driving profitability and long-term growth.

Charles' impact extends far beyond the corporate world. A passionate advocate for community engagement and leadership development, he serves on multiple boards and councils, including the Center for Children and Young Adults (CCYA), Fernbank Museum & Science Center Corporate Leadership

Council, 100 Black Men of South Metro Atlanta and the City of Smyrna's Committee to Honor Fanny Williams. As the founder and senior pastor of The Breakthrough Fellowship, he combines his professional expertise with a deep commitment to inspiring others to unlock their full potential.

A commanding presence on stage, Charles is a sought-after speaker known for delivering high-impact presentations at premier events such as the Detroit RIMS Chapter, COO Forum Atlanta, National Black MBA Conference, and Women in Insurance Conference. His thought leadership on growth strategies, innovation, insurance trends and leadership consistently empower audiences with actionable insights to drive meaningful change.

Charles Maxell, Jr., is not just an executive, he's a visionary force for progress. Whether transforming businesses or uplifting communities, he embodies excellence, purpose, and innovation at every turn. An author, devoted husband, proud father, and mentor to many, Charles inspires others to dream boldly and achieve extraordinary results.

NOTES

1 Proverbs 22:6 NLT
2 Psalm 55:12
3 John 14:12
4 1 John 3:1-3
5 Genesis 11:31
6 Unless otherwise noted, scriptures are taken from the New Revised Standard Version Updated Edition.
7 Genesis 11:27, 31-32
8 Isaiah 43:18-19
9 Acts 7:2-4
10 1 Corinthians 2:9
11 Mark 14:36 NRSV
12 Mark 14:36 NRSV
13 Genesis 12:1
14 In the immortal words of The Clash, "Should I Stay or Should I go"
15 Genesis 11:31-32
16 The gospel anthem "If I Can Help Somebody" was written by Alma Bazel Androzzo and first recorded and released by Billy Eckstine with Bobby Tucker and his orchestra in 1957. Sung by Mahalia Jackson.
17 Excerpt from Rev. Dr. Martin Luther King's speech, "I've Been to the Mountaintop"
18 Genesis 12:1-2
19 Genesis 12:1
20 Genesis 12:2
21 Genesis 12:1
22 Genesis 41:37-57
23 Nehemiah 1-6
24 Romans 8:31
25 Isaiah 54:17
26 Philippians 2:10-11
27 1 Samuel 17:32-37
28 Genesis 12:2-3
29 Genesis 11:31-32
30 *Hebrews 10:23*
31 Philippians 4:13
32 Inspired by the song, "Backstabbers" by the O-Jays
33 For those who don't know what "shout" means, it's the emotional, impactful moment of a sermon.

[34] Matthew 25:21,23

[35] Genesis 50:20

[36] Isaiah 40:31

[37] Psalm 30:5

[38] Psalm 23:1

[39] Psalm 23:4

[40] In the Bible, "strong tower" symbolizes God as a place of refuge and protection, especially for the righteous. It's a metaphor for God's unwavering strength and safety in times of trouble.

[41] Quote from Rev. Dr. Martin L King, Jr.

[42] Philippians 3:12-14

[43] Ecclesiastes 3:1

[44] Ecclesiastes 10:8, New Living Translation

[45] Scripture reference

[46] Genesis 50:20

[47] Ephesians 3:20

[48] Psalm 46:1

[49] Psalm 90:10

[50] Proverbs 18:10

[51] James C. Denison, 7 Crucial Questions About the Bible. Nashville: Broadman and Holman, 1994, p. 89-90.

[52] Jack Canfield and Mark Victor Hansen. A 2nd Helping of Chicken Soup for the Soul. Deerfield Beach, FL: Health Communications, Inc. 1994, p. 255.

[53] Charles Schultz, Good Grief. New York: Pharos Books, 1989, p. 201.

[54] Scripture reference

[55] Scriptural reference.

[56] Matthew 1

[57] Jesus is sometimes referred to as the "Balm of Gilead" because the balm of Gilead was a well-known healing substance in biblical times, and the image of the balm is used symbolically to represent Christ's ability to heal both physical and spiritual wounds.

[58] Hold to God's Unchanging Hand Jennie B. Wilson, pub. 1906

[59] Genesis 12:10-16 (Abram in Egypt): [10]Now there was a famine in the land, and Abram, went down to Egypt to live there for a while because the famine was severe. [11]As he was about to enter Egypt, he said to his wife Sarai, "I know what a beautiful woman you are. [12]When the Egyptians see you, they will say, "This is his wife." Then they will kill me but will let you live. [13]Say you are my

sister, so that I will be treated well for your sake and my life will be spared because of you."

¹⁴When Abram came to Egypt, the Egyptians saw Sarai was a very beautiful woman. ¹⁵And when Pharaoh's officials saw her, they praised her to Pharaoh, and she was taken into his palace. ¹⁶He treated Abram well for her sake, and Abram acquired sheep and cattle, male and female donkeys, male and female servants, and camels.

[60] Genesis 13:8-9
[61] Genesis 13:14-15
[62] Genesis 14:21
[63] Genesis 14:22-24
[64] Genesis 15:1
[65] Genesis 15:2
[66] Genesis 15:4
[67] Genesis 15:1
[68] In Genesis 17, God changes Abram's name to Abraham and Sarai's name to Sarah.
[69] Genesis 17:4-5
[70] Philippians 2:9-11